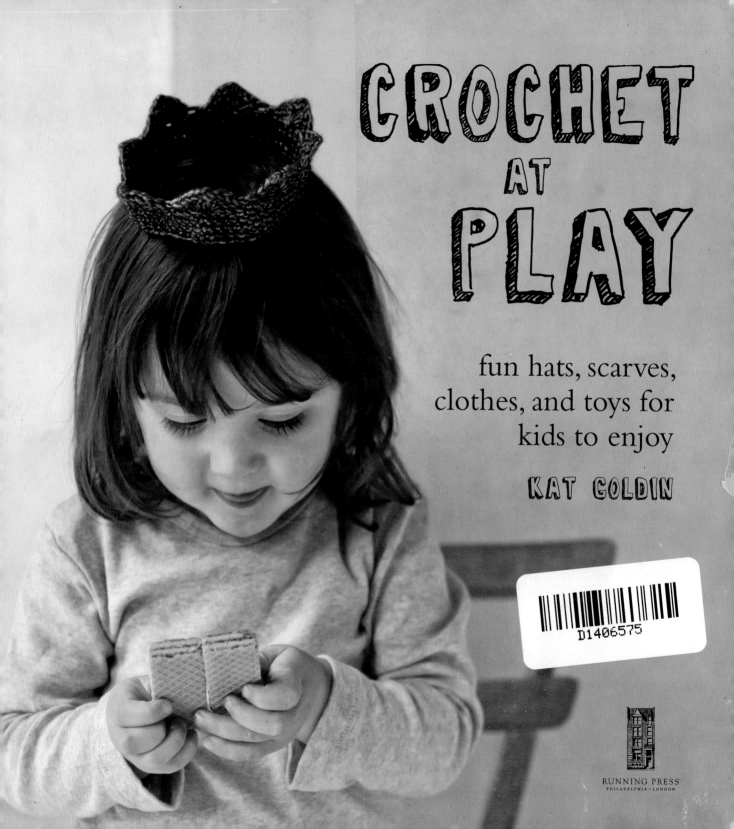

CROCHET AT PLAY

fun hats, scarves,
clothes, and toys for
kids to enjoy

KAT GOLDIN

Running Press
PHILADELPHIA · LONDON

D1406575

To my four loves. You inspire me every day.

First published in the United States in 2013
by Running Press Book Publishers
A Member of the Perseus Books Group

Books published by Running Press are available at special
discounts for bulk purchases in the United States by
corporations, institutions, and other organizations. For more
information, please contact the Special Markets Department
at the Perseus Books Group, 2300 Chestnut Street, Suite 200,
Philadelphia, PA 19103, or call (800) 810-4145, ext. 5000, or
e-mail special.markets@perseusbooks.com.

ISBN 978-0-7624-5100-5
Library of Congress Control Number: 2013935258

9   8   7   6   5   4   3   2   1
Digit on the right indicates the number of this printing

Text © Kat Goldin 2013
Photographs © Kat Goldin 2013
Design © Kyle Books 2013
Illustrations © Sarah Leuzzi 2013
Technical illustrations © Kuo Kang Chen 2013

Running Press Book Publishers
2300 Chestnut Street
Philadelphia, PA 19103-4371

Visit us on the web!
www.runningpress.com

Color reproduction by ALTA London
Printed and bound in China by Toppan Leefung Printing Ltd.

CONTENTS

INTRODUCTION

If you were to take the contents of this book and boil them down to distil the essence of the design, you would find that the chief ingredient of every item in the book is "fun." From the big picture of each chapter to the finer details of the wool, stitch, and construction choices, I have always tried to keep the fun-factor at the forefront of my mind:

- fun to make
- fun to wear
- fun to see

Making for children is one of the best excuses I know to bring a touch of whimsy and magic to designs. Small touches, like ears sewn onto the hood of a jacket, make a normal garment come alive as a thing of play.

Although I had been taught to crochet as a child, it was the birth of my son in 2007 that reignited my desire to pick up a hook. Every family member and friend received ill-fitting hats and scarves. As my skills grew, I struggled to find things I actually wanted to crochet. Searching for hours through books and on Ravelry, it was rare to discover patterns that were modern, gender neutral, and wearable. So, I took up knitting.

And I knitted—scarves and hats and blankets and sweaters. And the more I knitted, the more I missed the portability and flexibility of crochet. Knitting needles are easily whipped out of complicated cardigans by toddlers. Stitches are missed when one's attention is diverted elsewhere. Over time, I was called back to the hook. This time, instead of looking for patterns, I decided to make my own. Influenced by knitwear design, the vibrant handmade movement and my own three small children, I have always sought to take a fresh look at crochet and its possibilities.

The patterns collected in this book are organized into four chapters:

Heads and Shoulders, for hats, scarves, and capes

Fingers, Knees, and Toes, for gloves, slippers, and the like

Whole Self, for when you need something to put your "whole self" in (or at least the top half)

The Play Room, a collection of designs to liven up any space for children.

Most patterns in this book are sized up to age six, with a few just for the bigger kids and a few just for babies. From small, quick, last-minute gifts to bigger projects, this book has something for all of the small people in your life.

Happy crocheting (and most importantly, have fun!).

Kat
www.slugsontherefrigerator.com

GETTING STARTED

YARNS

When buying yarn, my advice is to buy the best you can afford. Children's items are small and require relatively little in the way of yarn, so it is a good excuse for paying a bit more for wool that will stand the test of time (and hand-me-downs) and will be enjoyable to wear and work with.

Walking into your local yarn or craft store, it is easy to be overwhelmed by the array of colors, fibers, and weights of yarn available. I have tried to choose yarns that not only look good, but also are relatively kid-proof, with a lot of washable choices and suggested alternatives.

Acrylic

There is no doubt that acrylic is the cheapest available. Inexpensive and often very soft, acrylic has become a go-to fiber for children's wear. However, acrylic yarns often don't wear well, and they can result in pilled and misshapen garments.

Wool

Scratchy wool jumpers from your grandma are a thing of the past (hopefully!) Wool yarns, especially merino wool, can be gorgeous and soft and light. There are many machine washable wool yarns on the market. Look for "superwash" on the label, particularly if you are making something as a gift. It means your lovingly handmade present is more likely to be worn. Superwash merino is one of my favorite fibers to work with.

Other Fibers

From cotton to bamboo to alpaca to milk fibers, there are an astounding number of yarns available. Cotton and bamboo yarns are excellent choices for children. They are usually machine washable and are great for layering. Other fibers each have their own properties. If you have questions about how a yarn will behave, ask a member of staff at your local store for advice.

Substituting Yarn

In each pattern throughout the book, I have suggested a yarn that works well for the pattern in terms of weight, drape, and washability. I have also given a few suggestions to help you find some other alternatives. In each pattern I have also included the amount of yarn required, the yarn's properties, and the weight. To ensure you are successful in substituting yarn, choose something similar.

HOOKS

Crochet hooks can be made from an endless variety of materials—wood, acrylic, aluminum, steel, to name a few. Personally, I prefer the glide and feel of aluminum crochet hooks, as they are both affordable and work with most yarns. However, it may take some time to figure out which kind you prefer, so try a few and see.

Crochet hooks are sized in relation to their diameter. A larger crochet hook will take more yarn into the stitch. Most of the time larger hooks are used with heavier yarn and smaller hooks with finer weights.

OTHER SUPPLIES

Tapestry/Yarn Needles

These have large eyes and are blunt.

Stitch Markers

Use the types that have a split ring or are open, as you will need to move them with each round. I often use just a scrap of yarn or a safety pin as a stitch marker, rather than buying anything special.

Sewing Needle

Used particularly for sewing on buttons. These are thinner and sharper than yarn needles. If you don't have co-ordinating thread for buttons, split your yarn lengthwise to thread through your sewing needle to sew on buttons.

Scissors

Sharp embroidery scissors are particularly useful for crochet, allowing you to make precision cuts without a lot of bulk getting in the way.

Buttons

Possibly my favorite part of making a garment is choosing the buttons. Remember that buttons can be choking hazards, so ensure they are sewn on very tightly and are checked regularly.

SIZING

All the finished garments in this book have detailed measurements. Each measurement has a guide for the age range the item will fit. Please remember that these are only guides, and that children come in all sorts of sizes. Use the actual measurements of the recipient to decide which "age" to make. The major measurements, such as chest and length, are given at the beginning of each pattern.

•   Head Circumference: Measure around head, just above their ears.
•   Chest: Measure around the child's trunk, under their armpits.
•   Sleeve Length: Measure from their shoulder to their wrist.
•   Length: Measure from the back of their neck to their waist.
•   Waist: Measure around their natural waist.
•   Hand Length: Measure from their wrist to middle finger.
•   Hand Width: Measure across the palm of the hand, just under their fingers.

•   Foot Length: Measure from their toe to heel.
•   Foot Width: Measure across the ball of their foot.

The finished chest measurement of a garment, such as a cardigan or jacket, should be 2–4in larger than the child's actual chest measurements. Hats should be slightly smaller than their head circumference and tend to fit a large range of head sizes.

If you are making for a baby that hasn't been born yet, think about when the baby is due to arrive and how old they might be when they need the item you are making. If in doubt, size up.

Items in this book are generally sized large to make sure that there is plenty of room to grow.

GAUGE

Everyone crochets slightly differently. Some people work very loosely, some more tightly. For items such as scarves and home accessories, gauge isn't that critical, as you will just end up with a slightly bigger (or smaller) throw. However, to ensure that your garments fit, you need to ensure you are working to the specified gauge.

At the most basic level, gauge is the number of stitches and rows in a 4in square. Each pattern in this book will give you the information as to how many stitches and how many rows (or rounds) it will take to make a 4in square with your selected yarn and suggested hook.

To see how your gauge matches with the suggested one, make at least a 4in square with the suggested hook in the indicated stitch pattern. Then, if you plan to wash your finished item (which will be in most cases), wash and block (see page 14) your swatch as you intend to wash your finished object. Let it dry completely and then measure your stitches and rows.

If you measure more stitches and rows in the swatch than the suggested gauge, switch to a larger hook. If you measure fewer stitches and rows in the swatch than the suggested gauge, switch to a smaller hook. Then, make another swatch and wash it, as you did the first to double-check your gauge.

TECHNIQUES AND BASIC STITCHES

HOLDING YOUR HOOK AND YARN

Crochet hooks are sometimes held like a pencil, with your forefinger and thumb placed over the flattened portion of the hook, and with the end of the hook coming out over your thumb. Hooks can also be held like a knife, with the end of the hook under your hand.

The yarn should be held in the opposite hand to the hook. It helps to thread the wool through your fingers to create a bit of tension and give you better control of your work.

It will take some time to find what is most comfortable for you. If you are just starting out, choose a project that uses a heavier weight yarn and larger hook to make it easier to get to grips with the basic techniques.

Hook held like a pencil

Hook held like a knife

SLIP KNOT

Leaving a 6in tail, take the yarn and make a loop, crossing the cut end of the wool under the ball end of the wool. Reach through the loop with your hook and catch the ball end of the wool with your hook. Pull through the original loop. Pull both ends of the yarn to tighten.

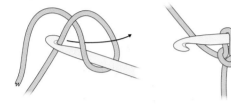

CHAIN STITCH (ch)

Begin with a slip knot on your hook and place your yarn over the hook. Twisting your hook slightly, draw your yarn through the loop on your hook. Repeat as many times as required.

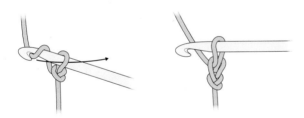

COUNTING CHAIN STITCHES

When counting how many stitches you have made, do not count the knot or the loop on your hook.

TURNING CHAINS

In order to get your new row or round up to the correct height, you will often be called to make a turning chain. These are chain stitches at the beginning of each row or round. Usually, you count the turning chain as a stitch, except in the case of single crochet. However, each pattern will tell you whether the turning chains are counted or not.

Crochet stitches are different heights. Each stitch has a corresponding number of turning chains made at the beginning of the round/row:

ch1 = Single crochet
ch2 = Half double crochet
ch3 = Double crochet
ch4 = Treble crochet

Sometimes you will be called on to chain more than the number required for the stitch, in which case that will count as a stitch plus a number of chains.

ANATOMY OF A CROCHET STITCH

Loops

At the top of the crochet stitch, you will see two strands, or a "V" that is left after you have made the stitch. Unless otherwise stated, always work into both strands.

Post

The "body" or "stem" of the stitch. This is the portion of the stitch that is made of yarn overs. The more yarn overs in a stitch means a taller post.

Fork

This is the bottom portion of the stitch that connects it to the previous round or row.

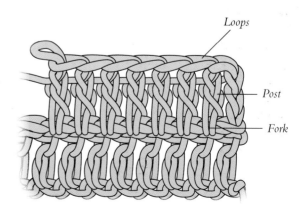

Loops

Post

Fork

SLIP STITCH (slst)

Slip stitches are most often used for joining rounds or for moving the working yarn to a new point on the garment without having to add bulky stitches or break the yarn.

1. Insert the hook into the stitch.
2. Place the yarn over the hook.
3. Pull through both the stitch and the loop on the hook.

Moving yarn

Joining in the round

SINGLE CROCHET (sc)

1. Insert the hook into the stitch.
2. Place the yarn over the hook.
3. Pull through the stitch.
4. Yarn over the hook again.
5. Pull through the two loops on the hook.

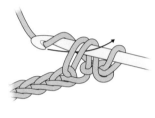

HALF DOUBLE CROCHET (hdc)

1. Place the yarn over the hook.
2. Insert the hook into the stitch.
3. Place the yarn over the hook.
4. Pull through the stitch (three loops on hook).
5. Yarn over the hook again.
6. Pull through all three loops on your hook.

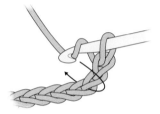

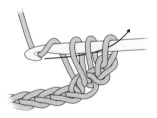

DOUBLE CROCHET (dc)

1. Place the yarn over the hook.

2. Insert the hook into the stitch.

3. Place the yarn over the hook.

4. Pull through the stitch (three loops on hook).

5. Yarn over the hook again.

6. Pull through two loops on your hook (two loops on hook).

7. Yarn over again.

8. Pull through the last two loops on the hook.

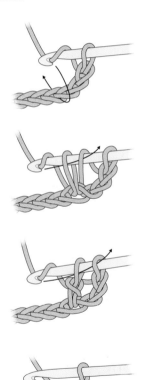

TREBLE CROCHET (tr)

1. Place the yarn over the hook twice.

2. Insert the hook into the stitch.

3. Place the yarn over the hook.

4. Pull through the stitch (four loops on hook).

5. Yarn over the hook again.

6. Pull through two loops on the hook (three loops on hook).

7. Yarn over the hook again.

8. Pull through two loops on the hook (two loops on hook).

9. Yarn over again.

10. Pull through the last two loops on the hook.

POST STITCHES

Post stitches are used in cable crochet and for making ribbing. They are made by working around the post/body of the stitch, instead of the top of the stitch. Post stitches can be made with any of the basic stitches, but are most often used with double crochet.

FRONT POST DOUBLE CROCHET (FPdc)

1. Place the yarn over the hook.

2. Insert the hook into the space between the stitch you are raising and the previous stitch, from the front of your work.

3. Bring the hook around the back of the stitch and through to the front of your work in between the stitch and the next stitch.

4. Yarn over hook.

5. Pull the loop back through the spaces between the stitches.

6. Yarn over and pull through two loops twice, as you would a normal double crochet.

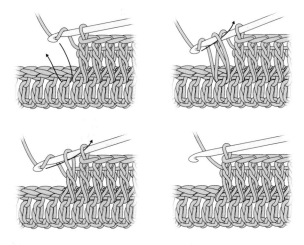

BACK POST DOUBLE CROCHET (BPdc)

1. Place the yarn over the hook.

2. Bring the hook to the back of your work and insert the hook into the space between the stitch you are raising and the previous stitch, from the back of your work.

3. Bring the hook around the front of the stitch and through to the back of your work in between the stitch and the next stitch.

4. Yarn over hook.

5. Pull the loop back through the spaces between the stitches.

6. Yarn over and pull through two loops twice, as you would a normal double crochet.

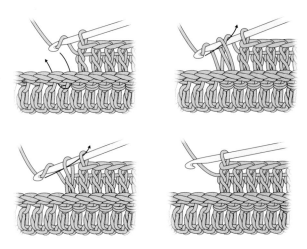

CABLED CROCHET

Cables are achieved in crochet by crossing groups of raised stitches. It can be tricky to understand at first. In all of the cables worked in this book, you will skip a specified number of stitches, work a group of raised stitches, then go back and work the skipped stitches so they cross over the front of the cable. You then continue working as normal in the pattern.

FOUNDATION SINGLE CROCHET (fsc)

Foundation crochet or chainless crochet is a way of working a starting row without having to work a chain. This is used in places where you need more stretch than a chain stitch can provide.

1. Starting with a slip knot, chain two.
2. Insert the hook back into the first chain.
3. Yarn over and pull through (two loops on hook).
4. Yarn over and pull through one loop on your hook (two loops on hook). This counts as your chain stitch.
5. Yarn over again and pull through the remaining two loops on the hook.

To continue:

1. Insert the hook into the chain stitch of the previous fsc.
2. Yarn over and pull through (two loops on hook). This counts as your joining stitch.
3. Yarn over and pull through one loop on your hook (two loops on hook). This counts as your chain stitch.
4. Yarn over again and pull through the remaining two loops on the hook.

DECREASES

Decreases are made by working the specified stitch up to the last yarn over, then inserting the hook into the next stitch, working it up to the last yarn over. Then yarn over and pull through all the loops on the hook.

WORKING IN THE ROUND

Of all the patterns in this book, most call for starting working in the round with a magic loop (also called adjustable loop). This is my preferred way of starting, as it enables you to get a very tight, closed first round.

1. Make a loop with the yarn, placing the cut end behind the ball end of the wool.
2. Reach through the loop with your hook, catch the ball end of the yarn with your hook, and pull through the original loop. Do not pull tight.
3. Chain the specified number of stitches. This will help secure the loop.
4. Make the specified stitches, working into the large loop at the bottom of your work.
5. Pull the tail end tightly to bring the bottom of the stitches into a circle.
6. After you have worked a few rounds of the pattern, tie off the tail end to prevent the magic loop from opening back up.

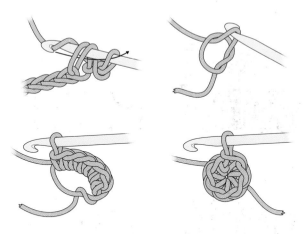

Alternatively, if you find the magic loop difficult, you can begin working in the round with four chains. Join with a slip stitch in the round and work your pattern into the loop created by the ring of chain stitched (not working into the individual chains, as you would when working flat).

JOINING YARNS

To join a new color or ball of wool seamlessly to your work, switch your yarn at the last yarn over of the stitch. For example, if I were switching when using single crochet, I would:

1. Insert the hook into the stitch.
2. Place the yarn over the hook.
3. Pull through the stitch.
4. Yarn over the hook again with the new color/yarn.
5. Pull through the two loops on the hook.

You can easily work in any ends of yarn by working around them as you continue down the round/row. Simply lay them across the top of the row you are working on and continue crocheting into the stitches as normal.

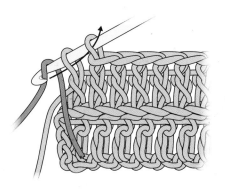

FINISHING

Once you reach the end of your work, cut the yarn, leaving at least a 6in tail for weaving in. Pull the cut end through the last loop that remained on your hook to stop your stitches from unraveling. If there are yarn ends that you have not been able to work in as described above, use a tapestry needle to weave the remaining ends securely into the back of your work. Weaving them into 3–4 stitches in 3–4 different directions will ensure they do not pop out later.

WASHING AND BLOCKING

Always use the ball band for your yarn as a guide to how to care for your final garment. Many will say "Hand Wash Only." However, if your machine has it, it is often OK to use a wool cycle on most handmade items. Test your swatch first!

When working with wools that have a high natural fiber content, you are able to block your project, which will help the yarn relax into the shape you have made. There are many different blocking techniques. Steam blocking uses an iron with a high steam setting. Gently press your work (not too hard or you will flatten the stitches).

I normally use wet blocking. This can take longer to dry, but does tend to give the most consistent results.

1. Wet your work in lukewarm water with a bit of wool wash in it.
2. Gently agitate your work (not too hard—you don't want it to felt!)

3. Rinse in cool water and gently press the water out.
4. Lay your work flat on a towel and roll up to get more water out.
5. Lay the item out on a flat surface. It may help to pin the edges down to help it stay in shape.
6. Leave to fully dry.

SEWING UP

Slip Stitch Seams

Using a slip stitch to join different parts of an object creates a very strong seam. Line up the stitches of the two pieces you are joining and insert the hook through all four loops of the stitches, yarn over hook, and pull through the two pieces you are joining and the loop on the hook. Repeat to the end of the seam.

EMBROIDERY

A few of the patterns in the book call for a small amount of embroidery and hand sewing.

Slip Stitch Embroidery (Surface Crochet)

Working on the outside of your work, insert the hook into the space between the crochet stitch you wish to work from. Bring the hook out into an adjacent space, in the direction you wish to work in. Yarn over and pull through. Insert the hook into the next space between the crochet stitch you wish to work from. Bring the hook out through an adjacent space, in the direction you wish to work in. Yarn over and pull through the stitch and the loop on the hook. Repeat as required.

Running Stitch

Thread a needle with yarn and work up and down through the crochet fabric with even spaces between the stitches.

Backstitch

Backstitch is similar to running stitch, except you will work a portion of the stitches back on themselves. Pull the stitch through the crochet fabric and then back into the underside behind where the thread came out. The needle is carried under the fabric to the point of the new stitch, where it is brought up again and back to where the thread was brought up on the last stitch.

READING A PATTERN

I like to think of patterns as reading a code. It can be tricky at first, but patterns are written using standard abbreviations for stitches and what to do. Know the code and you've got it!

Stitch or instruction	Abbreviation
Back Loop Only	BLO
Back Post	xxBPxx
Chain	ch
Chain Space	chsp
Decrease(ing)	dec
Double Crochet	dc
Front Loop Only	FLO
Foundation	xxCrochet fxx
Half Double Crochet	hdc
Increase(ing)	inc
Round(s)	rnd(s)
Single Crochet	sc
Skip(ped)	sk
Slipstitch	slst
Treble	tr
Starting Chain	stch
Stitch(es)	st(s)
Turning Chain	tch
Work 2 x Together	x2tog
Yarn Over	YO

Pattern Basics

Example: Rows 2 (4, 6) – 7 (9, 11, -): Ch1, [2sc in sc, 2sc] three times, 2 (3, 4, -) sc, *2sc in sc; rep from * to end. Join. Turn. 20 (21, 22, -)sc.

• Numbers in brackets relate to the instructions for the various sizes from smallest to largest, working left to right. Can be row or round numbers, stitch counts or repeats.

• The symbol "-" in place of any instruction for a particular size means that size isn't worked in that portion of the instructions.

• The instruction "2sc in sc, 2sc" means make two single crochet in the next single crochet stitch, then single crochet in the next two stitches.

• Instructions in square brackets are to be repeated a set number of times, as directed immediately following the second bracket. There may be variations relating to the size, in which case follow the appropriate number in normal brackets.

• When instructions are proceeded by a *, this means to repeat that sequence of stitches as many times as indicated, usually to the end of the round or row.

• "Join" means to join the round, unless otherwise instructed, by working a slip stitch into the first stitch of the round.

• "Turn" means to turn your work.

• The stitch counts at the end of the row tell you how many stitches you should have worked in that row or round.

HEAD AND SHOULDERS

Acorn
Crown
Flat Cap
Flower and Bud Hat
Flower and Bud Cowl
Fox Stole
Leafy Capelet
Shaggy Lion
Many-Ways Alice Bands
Witch/Wizard/Princess
Wrap Around

ACORN

Inspired by my own childhood collecting baskets of acorns from our oak trees. This deeply textured hat looks complicated, but a few basic stitches combined with a zigzag pattern make it an interesting, but simple make.

skill level: intermediate

Size	Baby	Toddler	4+ years
Finished circumference	12¼in	15in	18in
Finished height	5½in	6¾in	7½in
Yarn amounts	66yd	99yd	131yd

MATERIALS:
- 3½oz of Cascade 220 (100% wool), 220yd/hank, Vandyke Brown (7822)
- H8/5.00mm hook
- Tapestry needle

YARN REVIEW:
You would be hard-pressed to find a range of yarns with the color options that are available with Cascade 220. This worsted-weight yarn's good stitch definition and wearability make it an excellent option for outerwear.

YARN ALTERNATIVES:
Malabrigo Worsted
Quince and Co. Lark

GAUGE:
Work 15sts and 8 rows in double crochet to measure 4in square using H8/5.00mm hook, or size required to obtain gauge.

SPECIAL STITCH PATTERNS:
Puff Stitch (PS)
[YO, insert the hook into the stitch and draw up a loop] twice (five loops on hook). YO and pull through four loops on hook. YO and pull through last two loops on hook.

Pattern notes:

This is a very stretchy pattern where each size will fit a range of head sizes.

Do not turn your work at the end of each round.

INSTRUCTIONS:

Make 4ch. Join in the round.

Round 1: Ch4 (counts as 1dc and ch1), 2dc, [1dc, ch1, 2dc] four times. Join in 3rd ch of stch. [15 sts].

Round 2: (From Round 3 on, the ch2 at the beginning of the rounds do not count as a st) ch2, ★(PS, ch1, PS) in chsp, sk 1dc, 3dc in dc, sk 1dc; rep from ★ to end. Join into the 1st chsp. [25 sts].

Round 3: Ch2, ★(PS, ch1, PS) in chsp, 1FPdc in dc, 3dc in next dc, 1FPdc in next dc; rep from ★ to end. Join in the 1st chsp. [35 sts].

For sizes Toddler and 4+ years ONLY

Round 4: Ch2, ★(PS, ch1, PS) in chsp, 1FPdc in next 2 sts, 3dc in next dc, 1FPdc in next 2 sts; rep from ★ to end. Join in the 1stfirst chsp. [- (45, 45) sts].

For size 4+ years ONLY

Round 5: Ch2, ★(PS, ch1, PS) in chsp, 1FPdc in next 3 sts, 3dc in next dc, 1FPdc in next 3 sts; rep from ★ to end. Join in the first chsp. [- (-, 55) sts].

For ALL sizes

Round 4 (5, 6) – 9 (12, 15): Ch2, ★(PS, ch1, PS) in chsp; sk 1 FPdc, 1FPdc in the next 1 (2, 3) sts, 3dc in next dc, 1FPdc in the next 1 (2, 3) sts, sk one FPdc; rep from ★ to end. Join in the 1st chsp. [35 (45, 55) sts].

For size Baby ONLY

Round 10: ★(PS, ch1, PS) in chsp, 1FPdc, 3FPhdc, 1FPdc; rep from ★ to end. Join. Break yarn and weave in ends. [35 sts].

For size Toddler ONLY

Round 13: ★(PS, ch1, PS) in chsp, 1FPdtr, 1FPdc, 3FPhdc, 1FPdc, 1FPdtr; rep from ★ to end. Join. Break yarn and weave in ends. [45 sts].

For size 4+ years ONLY

Round 16: ★(PS, ch1, PS) in chsp. 2FPdtr, 1FPdc, 3FPhdc, 1FPdc, 2FPdtr★ rep from ★ to end. Join. Break yarn and weave in ends. [55 sts].

Stem (All sizes)

Make Ch2, 3sc into a magic loop. (4)

Rounds 1–4: (You will work in a spiral) 4sc. (4)

Fasten off, leaving a 11¾in tail. Using the tail, sew onto the top of the hat.

CROWN

A quick and easy make for your little royalty.

skill level: beginner

Size	Newborn	Baby	Toddler	4+ years
Circumference	12in	14in	17in	19in
Yarn amounts	21yd	29yd	41yd	50yd

MATERIALS:
- 1¾oz of Sublime Lustrous Extra Fine Merino (67% extra fine merino, 33% nylon), 104yd/ball Flinty (259)
- Also pictured 1 x ball of Sublime Lustrous Extra Fine Merino - Truffle (289)
- F5/3.75mm hook
- Tapestry needle

YARN REVIEW:
Soft and luxurious, this sport weight wool not only looks lovely, but also will make your little one feel like royalty.

YARN ALTERNATIVES:
James C Brett Twinkle DK

GAUGE:
Work 21 sts and 12 rows to measure 4in square using F5/3.75mm hook, or size required to obtain gauge.

PATTERN NOTES:
- This pattern can easily be sized up or down by altering the number of chain stitches in multiples of eight.
- Do not count the ch1 at the beginning of the round as a stitch.
- Do not turn your work at the end of each round.

INSTRUCTIONS:

Make ch 64 (72, 88, 96). Join in the round.

Rounds 1–4 (5, 6, 7): Ch1, 64 (72, 88, 96) sc. Join. [64 (72, 88, 96)sc].

Round 5 (6, 7, 8): (Ch3 (counts as 1dc), 3dc, ch2, 4dc) in sc, sk 3, 1sc, sk 3sts, ★(4dc, ch2, 4dc) in sc, sk 3 sts, 1sc, sk 3 sts; rep from ★ around. Join. [8 (9, 11, 12) double stitch clusters].

Break yarn and weave in ends.

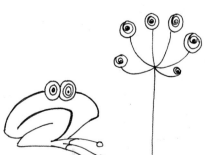

FLAT CAP

Perfect for walking out on the moors or toddling out at the park.

skill level: beginner

Size	Newborn	Baby	Toddler	4+ years
Circumference	13¾in	15¼in	16½in	18½in
Length	7in	7½in	8in	9in
Yarn amounts	52yd	59yd	77yd	90yd

MATERIALS:

◎ 1¾oz of Debbie Bliss Donegal Luxury Tweed Aran (90% wool, 10% Angora), 97yd/ball Chocolate (360014)
◎ H8/5.00mm hook
◎ G6/4.00mm hook
◎ Tapestry needle
◎ 12½ (14, 15¼, 17¼)in of fine elastic cord, tied or sewn into a loop

YARN REVIEW:

The touch of Angora in this tweed worsted weight yarn makes it a very soft and wearable yarn.

YARN ALTERNATIVES:

Rowan Felted Tweed Aran
Patons Soft Tweed Aran

GAUGE:

Work 14 sts and 10 rows in pattern to measure 4in square using H8/5mm hook, or size needed to obtain gauge.

PATTERN:

Row 1: Ch1 (does not count as a st), sc across.
Row 2: Ch3 (counts as 1dc), dc across. Line up working edge of the brim with the stitches not worked at the front flap of the hat, upside down, RS facing. Place your elastic loop on top of your work and work around it as you slst brim to the underside of the hat. This will help the hat stay on.

PATTERN NOTES:

• This hat has a slightly unusual construction. You will start at the front flap, working in rounds, then only work with half of the stitches in rows to the back of the head. You will join the brim on after the rest of the hat is complete.

- Count the ch3 at the beginning of dc rounds/rows as a stitch.
- Do NOT count the ch1 at the beginning of sc rounds/rows as a stitch.

Front Flap

With larger hook, ch 11 (11, 13, 15).
Round 1: Starting in the 2nd chain from hook, 2sc in the same ch, 8 (8, 10, 12)sc, 4sc in the last st, turning as you go to work in the other side of the chain, 8 (8, 10, 12)sc, 2sc in the first st (this stitch already has 2sc in it). Join in the first sc. [24 (24, 28, 32)sc].
Round 2: Ch3, 2dc in next st, 8 (8, 10, 12)dc, 2dc in next st, 2dc, 2dc in next st, 8 (8, 10, 12)dc, 2dc in next st, 1dc. Join. [28 (28, 32, 36)sc].
Round 3: Ch1, 2sc in tch of previous round, 2sc in next st, 8 (8, 10, 12)sc, 2sc in next st, 4sc, 2sc in next st, 8 (8, 10, 12)sc, 2sc in next st, 2sc. Join. [32 (32, 36, 40)sc].

For Newborn and Baby sizes, go to "Top" Section.

For sizes Toddler and 4+ years ONLY

Round 4: Ch3, 2dc, 2dc in next st, - (-, 10, 12)dc, 2dc in next st, 6dc, 2dc in next st, - (-, 10, 12)dc, 2dc in next st, 3dc. Join. [- (-, 40, 44)sc].
Round 5: Ch1, 4sc, 2sc in next st, - (-, 10, 12)sc, 2sc in next st, 8sc, 2sc in next st, - (-, 10, 12)sc, 2sc in next st, 4sc. Join. [-, (-, 44, 48)sc].

Top
For ALL sizes

This section extends half of the front flap stitches in rows to the back of the hat.
Row 1(RS): Ch3, 15 (15, 21, 23)dc. Turn. [16 (16, 22, 24)dc].
Row 2: Ch1, 1sc, 2sc in next st, sc to 2 sts from end, 2sc in next st, 1sc. Turn. [18 (18, 24, 26)]sc.
Row 3: Ch3, 2dc in next st, dc to 2 sts from end, 2dc in next st, 1dc. Turn. [20 (20, 26, 28)dc].
Rows 4–9 (11, 11, 13): Rep rows 2–3. Turn. [32 (38, 42, 48)dc].
Row 10 (12, 12, 14): Ch1, sc2tog across. Turn. [16 (19, 21, 24)sc].
Row 11 (13, 13, 15): Ch3, dc across. Turn. [16 (19, 21, 24)dc].
Row 12 (14, 14, 16): Ch1, 0 (1, 1, 0)sc, sc2tog across. Turn. [8 (10, 11, 12)sc].
Row 13 (15, 15, 17): Ch3, 7 (9, 10, 11) dc. Turn. [8 (10, 11, 12)dc].
Fold the last row in half, right sides together, lining up the stitches. Slst through all four loops along. Break yarn and weave in ends.

Brim

With smaller hook, ch 11 (11, 13, 15).
Row 1: Starting in 2nd chain from the hook, 10 (10, 12, 14)sc. Turn. [10 (10, 12, 14)sc].
Rows 2–4 (4, 6, 6): Ch1, 1sc, 2sc in next st, sc to 2 sts from end, 2sc in next, 1sc. Turn.
Row 5 (5, 7, 7) – 6 (6, 8, 8): ch1, 16 (16, 22, 24)sc. Turn. [16 (16, 22, 24)sc].

Line up working edge of brim with the stitches not worked at the front flap of the hat, upside down, RS facing. Slst brim to the underside of the hat.

Edging

Round 1: Continuing with the smaller hook and working around the elastic as you go, 26 (30, 30, 34)hdc around the underside edge of the hat back around to the brim, 1sc into every other row down the side of the brim, 10 (10, 12, 14)sc across the front of the brim, 1sc in every other row down the other side of the brim. Do not turn, do not join. [26 (30, 30, 34)hdc and 16 (16, 20, 22)sc].
Round 2: 6 (7, 7, 8)hdc, hdc2tog, 3 (4, 4, 5)hdc, hdc3tog, 3 (4, 4, 5)hdc, hdc2tog, 6 (7, 7, 8)hdc. Do not work in the brim. Break yarn and weave in ends. [22 (26, 26, 30)hdc].

FLOWER AND BUD HAT

Little clusters of puff stitches have always been my favorite crochet stitch. They remind me of springtime buds, just waiting to pop open.

skill level: beginner

Size	Newborn	Baby	Toddler	4+ years
Circumference	12in	14in	17in	19in
Height	4½in	5in	6¼in	7½in
Yarn amounts	50yd	65yd	96yd	126yd

MATERIALS:
- Main Color (MC): 1¾oz of Sirdar Simply Recycled DK (51% recycled cotton, 49% acrylic), 142yd/ball Grey (0018)
- Contrast Color (CC): 1 ¾oz of Sirdar Simply Recycled DK (51% recycled cotton, 49% acrylic), 142yd/ball Mustard (0019)
- F5/3.75mm hook
- Tapestry needle

YARN REVIEW:
The recycled cotton in this sport weight yarn is lovely and soft, making a perfect springtime hat.

YARN ALTERNATIVES:
Rowan Hand Knit DK Cotton
Wendy Supreme DK Cotton

GAUGE:
Work five pattern repeats and seven rows in pattern to measure 4in square using F5/3.75mm hook, or size required to obtain gauge.

SPECIAL STITCHES:
Puff Stitch (PS)
[YO, insert the hook in the stitch and draw up a loop] three times (seven loops on hook). YO and pull through six loops on hook. YO and pull through last two loops on hook.

Pattern notes:

Do not count the 2ch at the beginning of the round as a stitch.

Do not turn your work at the end of the rounds.

PATTERN:

[PS, ch2, PS] into the ch2sp between the PS cluster of the previous round.

INSTRUCTIONS:

Using MC, ch2, [PS, ch2] six times into a magic loop. Join. [6PS].

Round 1: Ch2, [(PS, ch2, PS) in ch2sp, (PS, ch2, PS, ch2, PS) in ch2sp] three times. Join. [15PS].

Round 2: Ch2, [(PS, ch2, PS, ch2, PS) in ch2sp, (PS, ch2, PS) in ch2sp twice] three times. Join. [21PS].

Round 3: [(PS, ch2, PS) in ch2sp three times, (PS, ch2, PS, ch2, PS) in ch2sp] three times. Join. [27PS].

For Newborn size, go to Row 7.

For sizes Baby, Toddler and 4+ years ONLY

Round 4: Ch2, [(PS, ch2, PS, ch2, PS) in next ch2sp, (PS, ch2, PS) in ch2sp four times] three times. [- (33, 33, 33)PS].

For Baby size, go to Round 7.

For sizes Toddler and 4+ years ONLY

Round 5: [(PS, ch2, PS) in ch2sp five times, (PS, ch2, PS, ch2, PS) in ch2sp] three times. Join. [- (-, 39, 39) PS].

For Toddler size, go to Round 7.

For size 4+ years ONLY

Round 6: Ch2, [(PS, ch2, PS, ch2, PS) in ch2sp, (PS, ch2, PS) in ch2sp six times] three times. [- (-, -, 45)PS].

For ALL sizes

Round 7: (For Newborn and Baby, work this round in CC, for Toddler and 4+ work in MC) ch2, (PS, ch2, PS) in each ch2sp around. [30 (36, 42, 48)PS].

Round 8: (For Newborn and Baby, work this round in MC, for Toddler and 4+ work in CC) ch2, (PS, ch2, PS) in each ch2sp around. [30 (36, 42, 48)PS].

Round 9: Rep round 7.

Round 10: Rep round 8.

For Newborn and Baby sizes, go to Edging.

For sizes Toddler and 4+ years ONLY

Round 11: Rep round 7.

For Toddler size, go to Edging.

For size 4+ years ONLY

Round 12: Rep round 7.

Edging
For ALL sizes

Round 1: Using MC, ch1, ★1sc, ch1, 1sc in ch2sp, sk 1; rep from ★ around. (Do not join. You will work in a spiral. Use a stitch marker to mark the beginning of the round.) [30 (36, 42, 48)sc].

Rounds 2–3 (3, 5, 5): ★1sc in next chsp, ch1; rep from ★ around. [30 (36, 42, 48)sc].

Break yarn and weave in ends.

Flower (Make 2)

Round 1: Using CC, ch2, 4sc into a magic loop. Join. [4sc].

Round 2: [(Ch3, PS, ch3, slst) in sc] five times. You will work the last petal in the same sc as the first petal. Break yarn, leaving an 8in tail for sewing. Using photo for placement, sew onto hat. [5 petals].

FLOWER AND BUD COWL

A complementary project to the Flower and Bud Hat, this cowl is made up of a pattern of puff stitch clusters and granite stitch.

skill level: beginner

Size	Small	Medium	Large
Circumference	18in	20in	22in
Height	5in	5in	6¼in
Yarn amounts	57yd	64yd	88yd

MATERIALS:
- Main Color (MC): 1¾oz of Sirdar Simply Recycled DK (51% recycled cotton, 49% acrylic), 142yd/ball Grey (0018)
- Contrast Color (CC): Small amount of Sirdar Simply Recycled DK (51% recycled cotton, 49% acrylic), 142yd/ball Mustard (0019)
- F5/3.75mm hook
- Tapestry needle

YARN REVIEW:
This sport weight yarn is light enough for cool spring and autumn days.

YARN ALTERNATIVES:
Rowan Hand Knit DK Cotton
Wendy Supreme DK Cotton

GAUGE:
Work five pattern repeats and seven rows in pattern to measure 4in square using F5/3.75mm hook, or size required to obtain gauge.

SPECIAL STITCHES:
Puff Stitch (PS)
[YO, insert the hook in the stitch and draw up a loop] three times (seven loops on hook). YO and pull through six loops on hook. YO and pull through last two loops on hook.

PATTERN:
[PS, ch2, PS] in the ch2sp between the PS cluster of the previous round.

Pattern notes:

This is a quick little pattern that can be made to many different variations, even sized up or down by simply chaining multiples of eight and adding or subtracting pattern repeats.

Do not count the chain stitches at the beginning of the round as a stitch.

Do not turn your work at the end of each round.

INSTRUCTIONS:

Using MC, ch 72 (80, 88). Join to work in the round.

Round 1: Ch1, ★1sc, ch1, sk 1ch; rep from ★ to end. Join. [36 (40, 44)sc].

Round 2: Ch1, ★1sc in chsp, ch1, sk next st; rep from ★ to end. Join. [36 (40, 44)sc].

Round 3: Ch3, ★sk [1sc, ch1, 1sc], [PS, ch2, PS] in chsp; rep from ★ to end. Join. [36 (40, 44)sc].

Round 4: Ch1, ★1sc, ch1, 1sc in ch2sp, sk 1sc; rep from ★ to end. Join. [36 (40, 44)sc].

Round 5: Ch1, ★1sc in chsp, ch1, sk 1sc; rep from ★ to end. Join. [36 (40, 44)sc].

Work rounds 2–5 four (four, five) times. Work round 5 one final time. Break yarn and weave in ends.

FOX STOLE

It came as a huge shock to me when I first moved to the UK that foxes aren't just adorable wild creatures that live in forests, but also pests that live in cities. I don't care and love them anyway.

skill level: intermediate

Size	Small	Medium	Large
Length	38¼in	40½in	43¾in
Yarn amounts	178yd	184yd	190yd

MATERIALS:
- Main Color (MC): 3½oz of Adriafil Regina (100% wool), 137yd (Rust 049)
- White: 1¾oz of Adriafil Regina (100% wool), 137yd/ball (White 01)
- Black: 1¾oz of Adriafil Regina (100% wool), 137yd (Black 02)
- You only need very small amounts of the white and black, so you may consider using yarn you already have in your stash.
- H8/5.00mm hook
- 2 x buttons (½in diameter)
- Tapestry needle

YARN REVIEW:
With a wide variety of colors and at a very affordable price, this superwash sport weight wool is perfect for making something that is going to keep little people warm and stylish all winter.

YARN ALTERNATIVES:
King Cole Merino Blend DK

GAUGE:
Make 6.5 sts and 10 rows to measure 4in square using H8/5.00mm hook, or size required to obtain gauge.

SPECIAL STITCHES:
Wattle Stitch
[Sc, hdc, dc] in same st, sk 2 sts.

PATTERN NOTES:
This scarf is sized only by adding length to the red section of the scarf, making it easy to size up to an adult length.

INSTRUCTIONS:

Fox Face

Starting with MC, ch2 (does not count as a st), 8hdc into a magic loop. Join. [8 hdc].

Round 1: Ch2, 2hdc in each st around. Join. [16 hdc].

Round 2: Ch2, [1hdc, 2hdc in next st] eight times. Join. [24 hdc].

Round 3: Ch2, [2hdc, 2hdc in next st] eight times. Join. [32 hdc].

Round 4: Ch2, [3hdc, 2hdc in next st] seven times, 4hdc, 4fsc, ch1, working down the other side of the fsc, 2sc in the first st, 3sc, 1hdc in the same st as the last hdc that was made. Join. Do not turn. [49 sts].

Round 5: Ch1, [4sc, 2sc in next st] twice, 5sc, 2fsc, ch2, working down the other side of the fsc, 2sc, 1sc in the same sc that you started the fsc from, 4sc, 2sc in next st, 5sc, 2fsc, ch2, working down the other side of the fsc, 2sc, 1sc in the same sc that you started the fsc from, [4sc, 2sc in next st] twice, 7sc, 2sc in next st, ch3, 2sc in next st, 5sc. Join. Do not turn. [66 sts].

Round 6: Ch1, [5sc, 2sc in next st] two times, 7sc, [1sc, ch3, 1sc] in ch2sp, 8sc, 2sc in next st, 7sc, [1sc, ch3, 1sc] in ch2sp, 8sc, 2sc in next st, 5sc, 2sc in next st, 8sc, switch to black, carrying the MC under the back as you go, 2sc in next st, [2sc, ch2, 2sc] in the ch2sp, 2sc in next st. Break black, leaving a 6in tail. Switch to MC, 6sc. Do not join. Do not turn. [81 sts].

Round 7: (Always carry the MC under your other colors as you work around and only break the CC where indicated.) Continuing with MC, 1sc, switch to white, [1sc, (1hdc, 1dc, 1hdc) in next st] five times, 1sc. Break white yarn, switch to MC, 7sc, switch to black, 2hdc, 1sc, (2sc, ch2, 2sc) in ch3sp, 1sc, 2hdc. Break black yarn, switch to MC, 13sc. Switch to black, 2hdc, 1sc, (2sc, ch2, 2sc) in ch3sp, 1sc, 2hdc. Break black yarn, switch to MC, 7sc. Switch to white, [1sc, (1hdc, 1dc, 1hdc) in next st] five times, 1sc. Break white yarn, switch to MC, 1sc. Break yarn and weave in ends. [91 sts].

Body

Using MC, ch18.

Row 1: Starting in third chain from hook (tch counts as 1hdc), [(1sc, 1hdc, 1dc) in next st, sk 2 sts] five times, 1hdc. [17 sts].

Rows 2–76 (82, 90): Ch2 (counts as 1hdc), [(1sc, 1hdc, 1dc) in dc, sk 2 sts] five times, 1hdc in tch. [17 sts]. You will carry the MC underneath the white, but drop the white when not in use.

Rows 77 (83, 91) – 78 (84, 92): With MC, ch2 (counts as hdc), [(1sc, 1hdc, 1dc) in dc, sk 2 sts] twice. Switch to white, (1sc, 1hdc, 1dc) in dc, sk 2 sts. Drop the white, switch to MC, [(1sc, 1hdc, 1dc) in dc, sk 2 sts] twice, 1hdc.

Rows 79 (85, 93) – 80 (86, 94): With MC, ch2, (1sc, 1hdc, 1dc) in dc, sk 2 sts. Switch to white, [(1sc, 1hdc, 1dc) in dc, sk 2 sts] three times. Drop the white, switch to MC, (1sc, 1hdc, 1dc) in dc, sk 2 sts, 1hdc. Break MC.

Rows 81 (87, 95) – 88 (94, 102): In white, ch2, [(1sc, 1hdc, 1dc) in dc, sk 2 sts] five times, 1hdc. Turn.

Row 89 (95, 103): 3slst, [(1sc, 1hdc, 1dc) in dc, sk 2 sts] three times, 1slst. Turn. [12 sts].

Rows 90 (96, 104) – 92 (98, 106): [(1sc, 1hdc, 1dc) in dc, sk 2 sts] three times, 1slst. Turn.

Row 93 (99, 107): 4slst, (1sc, 1hdc, 1dc) in dc, sk 2 sts, slst. Turn. [3 sts].

Rows 94 (100, 108) – 95 (101, 109): (1sc, 1hdc, 1dc) in dc, sk 2 sts, slst. Break yarn and weave in ends.

Back Legs (Make 2)

Using black yarn, ch5.

Row 1: Starting from 2nd chain from hook, 4sc. [4 sc].

Rows 2–12: Ch1, 4sc. Turn. [4 sc]. Break yarn, leaving a 6in tail for sewing up.

Front Legs (Make 2)

Using MC, ch5.

Row 1: Starting from 2nd chain from hook, 4sc. [4sc].

Rows 2–15: Ch1, 4sc. Turn. [4sc].

Rows 16–19: In black, ch1, 4sc. Turn. Break yarn, leaving a 6in tail for sewing up.

Finishing

Using the tail left on the end of the nose, fold the nose in half, lengthways. Make a small stitch where the back meets the MC to keep the nose folded in half.

Use MC for all the sewing so it does not show through the front of the scarf. Using the photo for placement, place your fox face on top of the straight edge of the scarf, lining up the scarf edge with the top of the white whiskers on the face. Make sure the head is centered on the scarf. Sew the face securely to the body at the scarf edge and add a few tacking stitches at the fox forehead and ears to keep secure.

Sew the front legs onto the back of the face, just below the line of the scarf. They should come out at a 45-degree angle from the head.

Sew the back legs on, approximately 2in up from the first row of white, again at a 45-degree angle to the body. Sew on the buttons for eyes, using the photograph for placement.

LEAFY CAPELET

Perfect for a walk in the woods to look for butterflies.

skill level: intermediate

Size	0-12 months	1 year	2 years	4 years	6 years
Finished length: bottom edge	36¼in	38in	40¼in	42in	44in
Finished length: shoulder to hem	11½in	12½in	13½in	14in	15½in
Yarn amounts	370yd	440yd	510yd	601yd	684yd

MATERIALS:

- 10½oz 10½oz 10½oz 14oz 14oz of Rowan Pure Wool Aran (100% superwash wool), 204yd/ball Forest (676)
- H8/5.00mm hook
- 2 x buttons (½in diameter)
- Tapestry needle

YARN REVIEW:

This lovely worsted weight superwash wool is even softer and more wearable after it has been blocked.

YARN ALTERNATIVES:

Debbie Bliss Donegal Luxury Tweed Aran

Sublime Cashmere Merino Silk Aran

GAUGE:

Work 12 sts and eight rows in HerrDc (see special stitches) to measure 4in square using H8/5mm hook, or size required to obtain gauge.

SPECIAL STITCHES:

Leaf

Ch4, dc3tog in base of chain.

Double Crochet 3 Together (dc3tog)

[YO, insert hook in stitch, YO, pull through stitch (three loops on hook), YO, pull through two loops] in three stitches. YO and pull through three loops. YO, pull through two remaining loops.

Herringbone Double Crochet (HerrDc)

YO, insert hook in stitch, YO, pull through stitch and first loop on hook, YO, pull through one loop, YO, pull through remaining two loops.

Herringbone Decrease (HerrDc2Tog)

YO, insert hook in the stitch, YO, pull

through stitch and first loop on hook, insert hook in next stitch, YO, pull through stitch and first loop on hook, YO, pull through two loops, YO, pull through remaining two loops.

Crab Stitch (crab)

(Also known as reverse sc.) Worked in the opposite direction to a normal sc (working from left to right). Insert your hook from front to back in next stitch to your right, YO, pull through stitch, YO, and pull through both loops on hook.

Pattern Notes:

• The cape is constructed from the bottom up, with the leaf edging made first.

• Stitches are then picked up along the long edge and a series of decreases are made up to the neck, where the hood is worked from the neck up.

• Count the chain stitches at the beginning of the row as a stitch.

INSTRUCTIONS

Leaf Border

Ch16.

Row 1(WS): 1dtr in 5th ch from hook (chain counts as 1dtr), make 1 leaf, sk 4 sts, 1sc, make 1 leaf, sk 4 sts, 2dtr. Turn. (4dtr, 1sc, 2 leaves).

Rows 2–35 (37, 39, 41, 45): Ch4, 1dtr, make 1 leaf, sk leaf, 1dtr, make 1 leaf, sk leaf, 2dtr. Turn. (5dtr, 2 leaves).

Row 36 (38, 40, 42, 46): Ch1 (counts as 1sc), 1sc, ch4, sk leaf, sc in dtr between the 2 leaves, ch4, sk leaf, 2sc. Turn. [5sc, 2 leaves].

With the yarn still connected, turn your work, WS facing, so you can work across the long edge of the leaf border.

Main Cape

Ch2 (counts as 1sc and ch1).

Row 1(RS): (this row is worked into the end of each row of the leaf border) [3sc, ch1] in the end of each row 36 (38, 40, 42, 44) times, 1sc in the beginning ch of the leaf border. Turn. [110 (116, 122, 128, 134)sc].

Rows 1–5 (7, 9, 11, 13): Ch3, 1HerrDc in each sc across. Turn. [110 (116, 122, 128, 134)HerrDc].

Row 6 (8, 10, 12, 14): Ch3, [4HerrDc, HerrDc2tog] 18 (19, 20, 21, 22) times, 1HerrDc. Turn. [92 (97, 102, 107, 112) HerrDc].

Rows 7 (9, 11, 13, 15) – 9 (11, 13, 15, 17): Ch3, 91 (96, 101, 106, 111)HerrDc. Turn.

Row 10 (12, 14, 16, 18): Ch3, [3HerrDc, HerrDc2tog] 18 (19, 20, 21, 22) times, 1HerrDc. Turn. [74 (78, 82, 86, 90)HerrDc].

Row 11 (13, 15, 17, 19): Ch3, 73 (77, 81, 85, 89)HerrDc. Turn.

Row 12 (14, 16, 18, 20): Ch3, [2HerrDc, HerrDc2Tog] 18 (19, 20, 21, 22) times, 1HerrDc. Turn. [56 (59, 62, 65, 68)HerrDc].

Row 13 (15, 17, 19, 21): Ch3, 55 (58, 61, 64, 67)HerrDc. Turn.

Row 14 (16, 18, 20, 22): Ch3, 2(3, 0, 0, 2)HerrDc, [2(2, 3, 3, 3)HerrDc, HerrDc2tog] 12 times, 5 (7, 1, 4, 5) HerrDc. Turn. [44 (47, 50, 53, 56) HerrDc].

Hood

Row 1: 9 (8, 9, 8, 9)slst, ch3, 25 (29, 31, 35, 37)HerrDc. Turn. [26 (30, 32, 36, 38) HerrDc].

Rows 2–6 (7, 8, 8, 9): Ch3, 25 (29, 31, 35, 37)HerrDc. Turn.

Row 7 (8, 9, 9, 10): Ch3, 2HerrDc in next st, ★1HerrDc, 2HerrDc in next st; rep from ★ across. [39 (45, 48, 54, 57) HerrDc].

Row 8 (9, 10, 10, 11): Ch3, HerrDc across. [39 (45, 48, 54, 57)HerrDc].

Row 9 (10, 11, 11, 12): Ch3, 0 (0, 0, 2, 3)HerrDc, [2HerrDc in next, 8 (20, 22, 7, 5)HerrDc] 4 (2, 2, 6, 8) times, 2HerrDc in next st, 1 (1, 0, 2, 4)HerrDc. Turn. [44 (48, 51, 61, 66)HerrDc].

Rows 10 (11, 12, 12, 13) – 15 (17, 18, 20, 21): Ch3, HerrDc across. [44 (48, 51, 61, 66)HerrDc].

Finishing

Do not break yarn. Fold the last row in half, right sides together, stitches aligned. Working through two stitches at a time, slip stitch the hood closed. Break yarn and weave in tails.

Edging

Turn the cape so it is upside down, right side facing. Attach the yarn so you can work across the edge of the leaf border first.

Round 1:

Work around the edge of the cape as follows:

4sc in the dtr that make up the end of the rows for the leaf.

Work each corner of the front of the

cape 2sc, ch2, 2sc.

Dc loosely in the end of each row up the front of the cape.

Make one button loop at the top of the front flap, one stitch down from the corner near the hood. Work as follows: make 5ch and slst in the next to last sc you just made (working backwards), work 5sc in the chsp.

Continue working sc around the hood and back down the other side, working another buttonhole as above on the opposite side of the front from the first. Join with a slst. Do NOT turn.

Round 2:

Work crab stitch around. Do not work crab in the buttonhole. Join. Break yarn and weave in ends.

Sew the button onto the opposite side of the cape from the buttonhole, in line with the hood edge.

Block the finished object to open up the leaf edge and help it lie flat.

SHAGGY LION

My daughter's first word was "Roar!" yelled at the top of her voice to anyone who would listen. It was only fitting I designed her suitable attire for such an activity.

skill level: beginner

Size	Newborn	Baby	Toddler	4+ years
Circumference	12in	14½in	17in	19¼in
Height	4½in	5in	6¼in	7½in
Yarn amounts	54yd	81yd	101yd	123yd

MATERIALS:
- Main Color (MC): 3½oz Rowan Cocoon (80% merino wool, 20% mohair), 126yd/ball, Amber (215) Contrast Color (CC): 3 ½oz Patons
- Shadow Tweed (56% wool, 40% acrylic, 4% viscose), Red, Burgundy, Orange (6906)
- I9/5.50mm hook
- Tapestry needle

YARN REVIEW:
A luxurious mix of wool and mohair, Rowan Cocoon is wonderful to work with. Combined with the wool for the mane this makes a very warm hat.

YARN ALTERNATIVES:
Wendy Mode Chunky
Twilley's Freedom

GAUGE:
13 stitches and 9.5 rounds in half double crochet to measure 4in square using I9/5.5mm hook, or size required to obtain gauge.

PATTERN NOTES:
- The hat is worked in the round until mid-forehead to keep the mane out of the face and eyes of the wearer.
- Switching then to rows, the back and sides of the hat are built up with stitches decreased in the very last row at the back to keep the bottom tucked in nicely.
- Earflaps are then built up on either side. The mane is tied on strand by strand.
- When working in the round on the top portion of the hat, do not count the ch2 as a stitch. When you switch to rows, it will be added to your overall stitch count.

INSTRUCTIONS:

Turn your work at the end of each round.

Using MC, Ch2 and make 8hdc into a magic loop. Join. [8 hdc].

Round 1: Ch2. *2hdc in each st around. Join. [16 hdc].

Round 2: Ch2, *1hdc, 2hdc in next st; rep from * around. Join. [24hdc].

Round 3: Ch2, *2hdc, 2hdc in next st; rep from * around. Join. [32 hdc].

Round 4: Ch2, *3hdc, 2hdc in next st; rep from * around. Join. [40 hdc].

For Newborn size, go to Round 8.

Round 5: Ch2, *4hdc, 2hdc in next st; rep from * around. Join. [48 hdc].

For Baby size, go to Round 8.

Round 6: Ch2, *5hdc, 2hdc in next st; rep from * around. Join. [56 hdc].

For Toddler size, go to Round 8.

Round 7: Ch2, *6hdc, 2hdc in next st; rep from * around. Join. [64hdc].

Rounds 8–9 (11, 13, 15): work even for 2 (4, 6, 8) rounds.

Back of Hat

Rows 1–3 (4, 4, 4): Ch2, 31 (35, 41, 47) hdc. Turn. [32 (36, 42, 48)hdc].

Row 4 (5, 5, 5): Ch2, 12 (13, 15, 17) hdc, hdc2tog, 2 (4, 6, 8)hdc, hdc2tog, 13 (14, 16, 18)hdc. Turn. [30 (34, 40, 46)hdc].

Earflaps

Row 1: Ch2, 9 (11, 13, 15)hdc. Turn. [10 (12, 14, 16)hdc].

Row 2: Ch2, 1hdc, hdc2tog, hdc to end. Turn. [9 (11, 13, 15)hdc].

Row 3 – (4, 6, 8, 10): rep row 2 until 7 sts remain.

Break yarn, leaving a 10in tail. Rejoin yarn at the first stitch of the last built up row at the front of the hat on the other side. Repeat the earflap from row 1.

Finishing

Edging

Starting in the bottom of one of the earflaps, right side facing, ch1 and sc around the edges of the earflaps and hat to ensure a nice even finish to the hat. This can be done in the wool for the mane or the hat.

Earflap Plait (Make 2)

Earflap plaits are made using six 12in lengths of yarn (MC and/or CC). Weave your tails from the earflaps through to the central space between the stitches at the bottom of your earflap. Thread the lengths of additional wool through the same spaces. Fold in half.

Using one length of wool, wrap around all of the tails and tie tightly, ensuring the strand is tucked under the wrap. Braid to desired length. Wrap and tie as above. Trim as required.

Mane

Using CC, cut lengths of wool approximately 5in in length.

Top Tip: To cut a lot of strips at once, wrap the yarn multiple numbers of times around your non-dominant hand. Cut through the top and bottom loops. Thread your hook through the spaces between the stitches. Fold length of mane in half and use your hook to pull through the gap in the stitches. Catch both cut ends in your hook and pull through the loop on your hook. Pull ends tightly to secure to hat. You'll need an approximately ½in wide strip of mane around the front of the face (slightly more on the top). Do not tie mane directly around the edging as you do not want fluff getting into your wearer's face.

Ears

Using MC, ch2, and 8hdc into a magic loop. Join.

Round 2: Ch2, *2hdc in each st; rep from * around. Join and break yarn. [16hdc].

(If the ears cannot be seen over the mane at this stage – add Round 3: Ch2, *1hdc, 2hdc in next st; rep from * around. Join and break yarn.)

Using the photos for placement, sew ears onto hat. Weave in ends.

MANY-WAYS ALICE BANDS

Who doesn't have 101 scraps of yarn lying around? These little projects only take small amounts of yarn and are quickly attached to store-bought Alice bands for a fun accessory or quick costume. In addition to the bow and the butterfly, you can also use the ear patterns from the Shaggy Lion hat and the Wolf jacket.

skill level: beginner

Type	Bow	Butterflies	Wolf Ears	Lion Ears
Width	4in	2in	2in	3in
Yarn amounts	296yd	10yd	12yd	9yd

MATERIALS:

For Bow
- 29yd of any sport weight yarn. Sample made in: Sirdar Snuggly Baby Bamboo DK (80% bamboo, 20% wool), 104yd/ball Coo (148)
- F5/3.75mm hook

For Butterflies
- 10yd of any sport weight yarn. Sample made in: Sirdar Snuggly Baby Bamboo DK (80% bamboo, 20% wool), 104yd/ball Cream (131)
- F5/3.75mm hook

For Circular Ears
- 9yd of any bulky weight yarn. Sample made in: Wendy Mode Chunky (50% wool, 50% acrylic), 153yd/ball Coffee Bean (218)
- Pipe cleaner or florist's wire
- J10/6.00mm hook

For Triangular Ears

- 12yd of any sport weight yarn. Sample made in Wendy Mode DK (50% wool, 50% acrylic), 155yd/ball Fog (232)
- Pipe cleaner or florist's wire
- G6/4.00mm hook

All

- 1 x headband (instructions included for both molded plastic and elastic varieties)
- Tapestry needle
- Hot glue (optional)

GAUGE:

Gauge is not critical to this project – a larger hook and yarn will make a larger accessory.

PATTERN NOTES:

In addition to these projects, you can also use the ears from the Wolf jacket and the Shaggy Lion hat. Go to the "Finishing" section for instructions on securing the ears to either a structured headband or a soft elastic one.

INSTRUCTIONS:

Sweet Bumpy Bow

With F5/3.75mm hook and yarn for the bow, ch 39. Join in the round.
Round 1: Ch1 (does not count as a st), working in the back bumps of the chain, 39sc. Join. Turn. [39sc].
Round 2: Ch1 (does not count as a st), 1sc, ★1sc, 1tr rep from ★ around. Join. Turn.
Round 3: Ch1, 39sc. Join. Turn.

Rounds 4–9: Rep rounds 2–3. Break yarn and weave in ends.

Finishing

Fold the tube in half so that the seam is at the back of your work. Gather the bow together at the middle and tie one end of yarn securely around the center to keep it gathered, leaving a 3in tail hanging. Wrap repeatedly, until the central wrap is approximately 1in in width. Cut the yarn and tie the newly cut end to the beginning tail. Use your crochet hook to hide ends inside the wrap.

Butterfly
Large

Using F5/3.75mm hook and yarn for the butterfly, ch1 (does not count as a st), [1sc, ch2] four times into a magic loop. Join. [4sc].
Round 1: Ch1, sk 1sc, 6tr in ch2sp, 1slst, [6hdc in ch2sp, 1slst] twice, 6tr in ch2sp. Join. Break yarn, leaving a 1½in tail for sewing. [24sc].

Small

With F5/3.75mm hook and yarn for the butterfly, ch1 (does not count as a st), [1sc, ch2] four times into a magic loop. Join. [4sc].
Round 1: Ch1, sk 1sc, 6hdc in ch2sp, 1slst, [6sc in ch2sp, 1slst] twice, 6hdc in ch2sp. Join. Break yarn, leaving a 1½in tail for sewing. [24sts]. Break yarn.

Abdomen

Cut a length of yarn for butterfly approximately 6in in length. Leaving a 2in tail at the top, wrap the yarn around the width of the butterfly three times and tie off the ends. Make a small knot at the ends of the tails to form the balls on top of the antennae and trim to size.

Finishing
Molded Plastic Alice Band

To secure the details on the moulded plastic band, thread a tapestry needle with matching yarn.
For the Flower/Butterfly: Position the item over a place where there are teeth in the headband on the opposite side. Work the needle through the back side of the wrapped yarn and into the underside of the item and down out again, making sure the needle does not come through the front side of the item. Wrap yarn around the plastic of the headband. Make several secure loops like this through the item and around the headband. Tie off. Using your crochet hook, pull the loose ends into the wrapped yarn. A dot of hot glue will help them stay in place.

Elastic Headband

To secure the details on the elastic band, thread a tapestry needle with matching yarn. (It may help to use a slightly sharper needle. If your yarn is too thick to be threaded through the eye, split the yarn ply apart or use matching thread or embroidery floss.)

For the Flower/Butterfly: Position item, work the needle through the back side of the wrapped yarn and into the underside of the item and down out again, making sure the needle does not come through the front side of the item. Then push needle through the elastic of the headband. Make several secure loops like this through the item and headband. Tie off. Using your crochet hook, pull the loose ends into the wrapped yarn. A dot of hot glue will help them stay in place.

Triangular Ears

Follow the pattern for the ears of the Wolf on page 113, up until the point of holding 2 together to join. Shape a small piece of pipe cleaner or florist's wire into a triangle, just smaller than ears. Place inside and sc around as indicated in the pattern.

Circular Ears

Follow the pattern for the ears of the Shaggy Lion on page 42, up until the point of holding two together to join. Shape a small piece of pipe cleaner or florist's wire into a circle, just smaller than ears. Place inside and sc around as indicated in the pattern.

Finishing
Molded Plastic Alice Band

To secure the details on the molded plastic band, thread a tapestry needle with matching yarn.

For the Ears: Position ears over a place where there are teeth in the headband on the opposite side. Push needle through the bottom of the ears, over the pipe cleaner and through the other side (the pipe cleaner should be between the sewing yarn and the headband) and then down around the plastic of the headband. Make several secure loops through the ears and around the headband. Tie off. Repeat for second ear. Using your crochet hook, pull the loose ends into the middle of the ear "sandwich." A dot of hot glue will help them stay in place.

Elastic Headband

To secure the details on the elastic band, thread a tapestry needle with matching yarn. (It may help to use a slightly sharper needle. If your yarn is too thick to be threaded through the eye, split the yarn ply apart or use matching thread or embroidery floss.)

For the Ears: Position ears, push needle through the bottom of the ears, over the pipe cleaner and through the other side (the pipe cleaner should be between the sewing yarn and the headband) and then down into the elastic of the headband. Make several secure loops through the ears, over the wire, and around and through the headband. Tie off. Repeat for second ear. Using your crochet hook, pull the loose ends into the middle of the ear "sandwich." A dot of hot glue will help them stay in place.

WITCH/WIZARD/ PRINCESS

Floppy, warm and made with Super Bulky wool your little magical creatures will be off making magic in no time.

skill level: beginner

Size	Newborn	Baby	Toddler	4+ years
Finished circumference	14in	15¾in	17¼in	20½in
Finished height	7¾in	10in	11in	12½in
Yarn amounts Wizard/Princess	32yd	37yd	48yd	68yd
Yarn amounts Witch	57yd	70yd	105yd	127yd

MATERIALS:
For Wizard
- 5¼oz Malabrigo Rasta (100% merino wool), 90yd/hank Azules (856)

For Witch
- 5¼oz Malabrigo Rasta (100% merino wool), 90yd/hank Black (195)

For Princess
- 3½ (3½, 5¼, 7)oz Sirdar Big Softie Super Chunky (51% wool, 49% acrylic), 45m Pink (347)
- 6.5mm/K10.5 hook
- Tapestry needle
- Stitch marker

YARN REVIEW:
This partially felted, Super Bulky wool works up quickly.

YARN ALTERNATIVES:
Seriously Chunky by Cygnet
Serenity Super Chunky by Wendy

GAUGE:
Work 7.5 sts and 8 rounds in single

Pattern notes:

This pattern is worked entirely in the round in the amigurumi style, with no seams or turning chains at the start of the rounds.

Use a stitch marker to mark the beginning of the round.

Do not turn your work at the end of the rounds.

crochet to measure 4in square using K-10.5/6.5mm hook, or size required to obtain gauge.

INSTRUCTIONS:

Ch1, 4sc into a magic loop. [4sc].

Round 1: *1sc, 2sc in next sc; rep from * around. [6sc].

Round 2: 6sc.

Round 3: *1sc, 2sc in next sc; rep from * around. [9sc].

Round 4: 9sc.

Round 5: *2sc, 2sc in next sc; rep from * around. [12sc].

Round 6: 12sc.

Round 7: *3sc, 2sc in next sc; rep from * around. [15sc].

Round 8: 15sc.

Round 9: *4sc, 2sc in next sc; rep from * around. [18sc].

Round 10: 18sc.

Round 11: *5sc, 2sc in next sc; rep from * around. [21sc].

Round 12: 21sc.

Round 13: *6sc, 2sc in next sc; rep from * around. [24sc].

Round 14: 24sc.

Round 15: *7sc, 2sc in next sc; rep from * around. [27sc].

Round 16: 27sc.

For sizes Baby, Toddler and 4+ years ONLY

Round 17: *8sc, 2sc in next sc; rep from * around. [30sc].

Round 18: 30sc.

For sizes Toddler and 4+ years ONLY

Round 19: *9sc, 2sc in next sc; rep from * around. [33sc].

Round 20: 33sc.

For size 4+ years ONLY

Round 21: *10sc, 2sc in next sc* rep from * around [36sc].

Round 22: 36sc.

Round 23: *11sc, 2sc in next sc; rep from * around [39sc].

Round 24: 39sc.

For ALL sizes

Work 4 (4, 5, 6) rows even. Finish off for the Wizard and Princess variations, or continue to Brim section for Witch variation.

Brim for Witch's Hat

Round 1: (working into FLO) *2sc, 2sc in next sc; rep from * around. [36 (40, 44, 52)sc].

Round 2: *3sc, 2sc in next sc; rep from * around. [45 (50, 55, 65)sc].

Round 3: *4sc, 2sc in next sc; rep from * around. [54 (60, 66, 78)sc].

Round 4: *5sc, 2sc in next sc; rep from * around. [63 (70, 77, 91)sc].

For sizes Newborn and Baby ONLY

Break yarn and weave in ends.

For sizes Toddler and 4+ years ONLY

Round 5: 2sc in next sc, - (-, 42, 44)sc, 2sc in next sc, sc to end. [- (-, 88, 104)sc].

Round 6: 2sc in next sc, - (-, 43, 45)sc, 2sc in next sc, sc to end [- (-, 99, 117)sc].

Break yarn and weave in ends.

WRAP AROUND

A sweet little shawl, perfect for dressing up or keeping warm, or both.

skill level: beginner

Size	0–12 months	1 year	2 years	4 years	6 years
Finished length	78in	85cm	100in	113in	121in
Yarn amounts	108yd	154yd	178yd	202yd	233yd

MATERIALS:
- 1¾ (3½, 3½, 3½, 3½)oz of Sublime Baby Cashmere Merino Silk DK (75% extra fine merino, 20% silk, 5% cashmere), 127yd/ball Pebble (006)
- G6/4.00mm hook
- 2 x buttons (¼–½in diameter)
- Tapestry needle

YARN REVIEW:
The drape and softness of this sport weight silk-blend yarn is simple, yet gorgeous.

YARN ALTERNATIVES:
Debbie Bliss Cashmerino DK
Rowan Cashsoft DK

GAUGE:
Work 18 sts and seven rows in double crochet to measure 4in square using G6/4mm hook, or size required to obtain gauge.

SPECIAL STITCHES:
Puff Stitch (PS)
[YO, insert hook into stitch and draw up a loop] three times (seven loops on hook). YO and pull through six loops on hook. YO and pull through last two loops on hook.

Pattern notes:

This shawl is constructed from side to side. Increases are only worked on the side next to the cable and puff pattern, giving it a long, shallow shape.

INSTRUCTIONS:

Count the ch3 at the beginning of each row as a stitch.

Ch9.

Row 1 (RS): Starting in 4th ch from hook (counts as 1dc), 2dc, sk ch1, [1PS, ch1, 1PS] in next ch, sk ch1, 1dc. Turn. [6sts].

Row 2: Ch3, [1PS, ch1, 1PS] in chsp between the 2 PS, 1BPtr in next dc, 2dc in next dc, 1dc in tch. Turn. [7sts].

Row 3: Ch3, 1dc, 2dc in next dc, 1FPtr, [1PS, ch1, 1PS] in chsp between the 2 PS, 1FPtr around tch. Turn. [8sts].

Row 4: Ch3, [1PS, ch, 1PS] in chsp between the 2 PS, 1BPtr, 2dc in next dc, 3dc. Turn. [9sts].

Repeat rows 3–4 8 (10, 11, 12, 13) times until you have 25 (29, 31, 33, 35) sts.

Rows 21 (25, 27, 29, 31) – 29 (35, 37, 43, 47): Work even.

Decreasing

Row 1: Ch3, 18 (21, 24, 26, 28)dc, dc2tog, 1FPtr, [1PS, ch1, 1PS] in chsp between the 2PS, FPtr around tch. [24 (28, 30, 32, 34 sts)].

Row 2: Ch3, [1PS, ch1, 1PS] in chsp between the 2PS, 1BPtr, dc2tog, 18 (21, 24, 26, 28)dc. Turn. [23 (27, 29, 31, 33) sts].

Repeat rows 1–2 8 (10, 11, 12, 13) times. Work row 1 once. [6 sts remain].

Cut yarn and weave in ends.

Edging

With RS facing, join the yarn on the short edge of the wrap.

Ch1, 4sc, turn, ch4, slst in 2nd sc made, turn, 5sc into the loop, continue working into the short edge 1sc, [1sc, ch2, 1sc] in the corner st, continue to sc along the long straight edge [1sc, ch2, 1sc] in the corner st, 4sc, turn, ch4, slst in the 2nd sc made, turn, 5sc in the loop, 2sc in the short edge. Break yarn and weave in ends.

Using your child as a guide for their placement, sew buttons onto the back of shawl, on the inside, in line with the edging.

FINGERS, KNEES, AND TOES

Baby Ballet Slippers
Beastie Feet
Sunshine and Showers Mittens
Glass Slippers
Hedgehog Mittens
Leg Warmers
Mermaid Tail
Tutu

BABY BALLET SLIPPERS

Delicate little ballet slippers for delicate baby feet.

skill level: intermediate

Size	Extra small	Medium	Large	Extra large
Foot width	2in	2¼in	2¼in	2½in
Foot length	3½in	4in	4¼in	5in
Yarn amounts	36yd	45yd	52yd	64yd

MATERIALS:
- 1¾oz of Sirdar Snuggly Baby Bamboo DK (80% bamboo, 20% wool), 95m Flip Flop (125)
- G6/4.00mm hook
- 2 x 7½ (7¾, 8¼, 9½)in of thin elastic cord or doubled shirring elastic tied or sewn into a loop
- 2 x 7in ribbon for ties
- Embroidery needle

YARN REVIEW:
Silky and drapey, this is a fabulous yarn to add a bit of sheen to your slippers.

YARN ALTERNATIVES:
Sublime Cashmere Merino Silk DK

GAUGE:
Work 17 sts and 23 rows in single crochet to measure 4in square using G6/4mm hook, or size required to obtain gauge.

NOTE ON SIZING:
These are sized up to approximately age two.

Pattern note:
Turn your work at the end of each round.

INSTRUCTIONS:

Toe

ch1, 4sc into a magic loop. Join. Turn. [4sc].

Round 1: Ch1 (does not count as a st), 2sc in each st around. Join. [8sc].

Round 2: Ch1, ★1sc, 2sc in next sc; rep from ★ to end. Join. [12sc].

Round 3: Ch1, ★2sc, 2sc in next sc; rep from ★ to end. Join. [16sc].

Round 4: Ch1, ★3sc, 2sc in next sc; rep from ★ to end. Join. [20sc].

For sizes Medium, Large, and Extra large ONLY

Round 5: Ch1, ★4sc, 2sc in next sc; rep from ★ to end. Join. [- (24, 24, 24)sc].

For size Extra large ONLY

Round 6: Ch1, ★5sc, 2sc in next sc; rep from ★ to end. Join. [- (-, -, 28)sc].

For ALL sizes

Work even for 2 (3, 3, 3) rounds.

Sole

Set-up: 7 (9, 9, 11)slst. Turn to move the line of joined stitches to the bottom of the sole.

Rows 1–13 (15, 16, 18): With WS (RS, WS, RS) facing ch1, 15 (19, 19, 22)sc. Turn. [15 (19, 19, 22)sc].

Fold the last row in half, right sides together, lining up the stitches; slst through all four loops along. Break yarn and weave in ends.

Edging

You are going to work around the elastic as you dc the edging. This will help the slipper stay on.

Round 1: Re-attach yarn at the top of the slipper, at the back where the slst seam is. Working around the elastic, ch1, 31 (35, 39, 44)sc, 6ch, 1sc in the same stitch to form a loop. Break yarn and weave in ends.

Finishing

Thread the length of ribbon through the loop at the back.

BEASTIE FEET

Fact: Slippers with claws are a childhood requirement.

skill level: intermediate

Size	0–6 months	6–12 months	1 year	2 years	4 years	6 years
Foot width	2in	2in	2in	2¼in	2½in	2½in
Foot length	3½in	4in	4¼in	5in	6¼in	6½in
Yarn amounts	30yd	37yd	41yd	50yd	63yd	70yd

MATERIALS:
- Main Color (MC): 8¾oz of Cascade Eco+ (100% Peruvian wool), 274yd Night Vision (8025)
- Contrast Color (CC): Small amount of Cascade 220 (100% Peruvian wool), Black (8555)
- G6/4.00mm hook
- J10/6.00mm hook
- K10.5/6.50mm hook
- 4¾ (5½, 6, 6, 6¼, 7)in of ⅜in wide elastic webbing
- Tapestry needle

YARN REVIEW:
Excellent value for money, one hank of this tweedy, bulky weight yarn will make slippers for the whole family.

YARN ALTERNATIVES:
Wendy Mode Chunky

GAUGE:
Work 15 sts and eight rounds in half double crochet to measure 4in square using a J10/6.00mm hook, or size required to obtain gauge.

SPECIAL STITCHES:
Slip Stitch Ribbing
Slst in BLO. This can be tricky to get to begin with, so just ensure you are crocheting loosely.

Pattern notes:

Of all of the crochet slippers I have made and worn over the years, those with a double sole are by far the most comfortable and worth the extra effort. The crochet soles are made first, then attached in pairs. The heel is worked directly onto the soles, then the top of the slipper is constructed separately then sewn on.

Chain stitches at the beginning of the rows and rounds. Do not count, unless otherwise stated.

INSTRUCTIONS:

Soles (Make 4)

Using the middle-sized hook and MC, ch 7 (9, 10, 11, 13, 15).

Round 1: 2hdc in 3rd ch from hook, 3 (5, 6, 7, 9, 11)hdc, 7 (8, 7, 7, 7, 8) hdc in last st, turning your work as you go to work in the other side of chain, 3 (5, 6, 7, 9, 11)hdc, 2hdc in last st (this is the same stitch that you made 2hdc in at the beginning of the round). Join. Do not turn. [17 (22, 23, 25, 29, 34)hdc].

For sizes 0–6 months and 6–12 months ONLY

Round 2: Ch1, [2sc in hdc] twice, 3 (5, -, -, -, -)sc, [2sc in hdc] 7(8, -, -, -, -) times, 3 (5, -, -, -, -)sc, [2sc in hdc] twice. Join. Do not turn. [28, (34, -, -, -, -)sc].

For sizes 1 year, 2 years, 4 years and 6 years ONLY

Round 2: Ch1, [2sc in hdc] twice, -(-, 3, 4, 5, 6)sc, - (-, 3, 3, 4, 5)hdc, [2sc in hdc] - (-, 8, 7, 7, 8) times, - (-, 3, 3, 4, 5)hdc, - (-, 3, 4, 5, 6)sc, [2sc in hdc] twice. Join. Do not turn.[- (-, 34, 36, 40, 46)sts].

For ALL sizes

Round 3: Ch1, 3sc, 2sc in next sc, 3 (5, 6, 7, 9, 11)sc, [2sc in next st, 1sc] 7 (8, 7, 7, 7, 8) times, 3 (5, 6, 7, 9, 11)sc, 2sc in next sc, 3sc. Join. Do not turn. [37 (44, 43, 45, 49, 56)sc].

Hold two soles wrong sides together and slst together through the BLO (these are the two inner loops in the "sandwich"). Cut the yarn and weave in the ends.

Heels

Row 1: Find the central backstitch of the soles (the one where the slst joined the last round of the sole). Count 8 (9, 9, 9, 11, 11) stitches towards the toe. Working into the unworked loop of the top sole inside facing, ch1, 17 (19, 19, 19, 23, 23)sc towards the centre back. Turn. [17 (19, 19, 19, 23, 23)sc].

Row 2: Ch1, 17 (19, 19, 19, 23, 23)sc. Turn. [17 (19, 19, 19, 23, 23)sc]. Work 0 (0, 0, 1, 2, 4) rows even.

Row 3 (3, 3, 4, 5, 7): Ch1, 2sc, sc2tog, 9 (11, 11, 11, 15, 15)sc, sc2tog, 2sc. Turn. [15 (17, 17, 17, 21, 21)sc].

Row 4 (4, 4, 5, 6, 8): (Tie or sew the elastic in a loop. You will work around the elastic for this last round.) Ch1, 15 (17, 17, 17, 21, 21)sc. Break yarn and weave in ends.]15 (17, 17, 17, 21, 21)sc].

Front Uppers (Make 2)

Using the largest hook and MC, ch9 (11, 12, 13, 15, 16).

Row 1 (RS): (Working in the back bumps of the chain) starting in 2nd chain from hook, 8 (10, 11, 13, 14, 15)slst. Turn. [8 (10, 11, 13, 14, 15)slst].

Row 2: Ch1, 8 (10, 11, 13, 14, 15)slst BLO. Turn. [8 (10, 11, 13, 14, 15)slst].

Row 3: Ch2. Starting in 2nd ch from hook, 9 (11, 12, 13, 15, 16)slst BLO. Turn. [9 (11, 12, 13, 15, 16)slst].

Rows 4–10 (14, 14, 18, 20, 24): Ch1, 9 (11, 12, 13, 15, 16)slst BLO. Turn. [9 (11, 12, 13, 15, 16)slst].

Row 11 (15, 15, 19, 21, 25): Ch1, 8 (10, 11, 13, 14, 15)slst BLO. Miss 1 st. Turn. [8 (10, 11, 13, 14, 15)slst].

Row 12 (16, 16, 20, 22, 26): Ch1, 8 (10, 11, 13, 14, 15)slst BLO. Turn.

Edging and Sewing on Upper

Row 1 (WS): Using the smallest hook, sc around 3 edges of the upper (not the top, straight edge), as follows:
Working down the sides, work through both loops of the slst ribbing.
Working the curved bottom edge, sc in every other row.
22 (28, 30, 36, 39, 43)sc.
Turn.

Row 2 (RS): Place upper on top of toe end of slipper, RS up. Line up the curved edge with the toe of the soles. Overlap the straight edge of the upper with the front side of the heel by 2 (3, 4, 5, 5, 6) stitches. Sew the upper onto the soles of the shoe, working around the posts of the sc edging and through both layers of sole. (You can also slip stitch the uppers in place, using the unworked

loop on the upper sole.) To keep the top straight, it may help to pin it in place as you work.

Row 3: Re-attach yarn to work across the straight edge of upper. Working in every other row, 2 (3, 3, 4, 4, 5)sc, 2 (2, 2, 2, 3, 3)sc working around the elastic that remains uncovered from the heel section, 2 (3, 3, 4, 4, 5)sc. Break yarn. [6 (8, 8, 10, 11, 13)sc].

Claws (Make 2)

Using the smallest hook and the yarn for the claws, [ch4, starting with the 2nd chain from hook, 1sc, 1hdc, 1dc] four times. Lightly block or steam iron to help the claws lie flat. Sew onto the front of the slipper.

SUNSHINE AND SHOWERS MITTENS

Convertible mittens are just perfect for kids, with the flexibility to keep little fingers warm, but still allowing them to explore and play.

skill level: beginner

Size	Small	Medium	Large
Circumference	4½in	5½in	6½ in
Length	4¼in	5¾in	6¾in
Yarn amounts	72yd	109yd	150yd

MATERIALS:

- Main Color (MC): 3½oz of Cascade 220 (100% Peruvian wool), 220yd/hank Silver Grey (8401)
- A small amount of Cascade 220 (100% Peruvian wool), 201m in the following colors:
  Cloud: Charcoal (8400)
  Sun: Sunflower (2415)
  Sun rays: Orange Sherbet (7825)
  Rain: Blueberry (9464)
  Rainbow: Colors as above, plus:
    Christmas Red (8895) and
    Christmas Green (8894)
- G6/4.00mm hook
- 7/4.5mm hook
- 2 x buttons (½in in diameter)
- Tapestry needle
- Stitch marker

YARN REVIEW:

Cascade 220 is a versatile worsted weight wool, comes in a huge range of colors and has excellent stitch definition.

YARN ALTERNATIVES:
Quince and Co. Lark

GAUGE:
Work 15.5 sts and 18 rows in single crochet to measure 4in square using a G6/4.5mm hook, or size required to obtain gauge.

SPECIAL STITCHES:
Foundation Half Double Crochet (fhdc)
First stitch:
Ch2, YO hook, insert hook in the first chain, YO and pull through stitch (three loops on hook). This is the joining stitch. YO and pull through first loop on hook (three loops on hook). This is the "chain" stitch. YO and pull through all three loops on hook.

Following Stitches:
YO hook, insert hook in the "chain" from the previous stitch, YO and pull through stitch (three loops on hook). This is the joining stitch. YO and pull through first loop on hook (three loops on hook). This is the 'chain' stitch. YO and pull through all three loops on hook.

PATTERN NOTES:

- Do not count the chains at the beginning of the round as a stitch.
- Do not turn your work at the end of each round.

INSTRUCTIONS:

(Make 2, but follow the instructions for Left and Right Mitten)

Round 1: With smaller hook and MC, make 18 (22, 26)fhdc. Join in the round. 18 (22, 26)fhdc.

Rounds 2–4 (5, 6): Ch3, ★FPdc, BPdc; rep from ★ to end. Join.

Rounds 5 (6, 7) – 8 (10, 11): Switch to larger hook, ch1, 18 (22, 26)sc. Join.

Thumbhole – Left Mitten

Round 9 (11, 12): Ch1 (does not count as a st), 1sc, 3 (4, 5)ch, sk 3 (4, 5) sts, 14 (17, 20)sc. Join in the first chain of the thumbhole at the beginning of the round. [15 (18, 21)sc].

Thumbhole – Right Mitten

Round 9 (11, 12): Ch1, 14 (17, 20)sc, 3 (4, 5)ch, sk 3 (4, 5) sts, 1sc. Join. [15 (18, 21)sc].

Both Mittens

Round 10 (12, 13): Ch1, 18 (22, 26)sc, working in just one loop of the chain stitches when you come across them. Join. [18 (22, 26)sc].

Rounds 11 (13, 14) – 13 (16, 18): Ch1, 18 (22, 26)sc. Join.

Flap Set-up – Left Mitten

Round 14 (17, 19): Ch1, 4 (5 ,6)sc, 7

(9, 11)sc in BLO (it may be useful to mark the unworked loops with a stitch marker so you can find them easily again), 7 (8, 9)sc in both loops. Join. [18 (22, 26)sc].

Flap Set-up – Right Mitten

Round 14 (17, 19): Ch1, 7 (8, 9)sc, 7 (9, 11)sc in BLO (it may be useful to mark the unworked loops with a stitch marker so you can find them easily again), 4 (5, 6)sc in both loops. Join. [18 (22, 26)sc].

Both Mittens

Rounds 15 (18, 20) – 17 (20, 23): Ch1, 18 (22, 26)sc. Join. Break yarn.

Flap

Round 1: Join yarn to the first unworked loop of round 14 (17, 19) of the mitten, RS facing. Ch1, 7 (9, 11)sc in free loops of the mitten, then 13

(15, 17)ch. Join to first sc of the round. 7 (9, 11)sc and 13 (15, 17)ch

Rounds 2–3 (4, 6): 7 (9, 11)sc across the sc and 13 (15, 17)sc in the ch. Join. [20 (24, 27)sc].

Round 4 (5, 7): Ch1, sc2tog ten (twelve, fourteen) times. Join. [10 (12, 14)sc].

Round 5 (6, 8): Ch1, 10 (12, 14)sc. Join.

Round 6 (7, 9): Ch1, sc2tog 5 (6, 7) times. Do not join. [5 (6, 7)sc].

Button Loop

Ch4, sk 2 (3, 3)sc, 1slst. Break yarn and pull through, leaving a 6in tail past the chain. Using a tapestry needle, sew the top of the mitten closed by weaving the yarn in and out of the last 5 (6, 7) stitches, pulling them tight to close, but leaving the ch4 loose at the top to act as a button loop. Tie off end.

Thumb

Round 1: Rejoin yarn at the skipped stitches at the thumb opening, ch1, 6 (8, 10)sc around, working in the skipped stitches and the unworked side of the chain. Join. [6 (8, 10)sc].

Rounds 2–4 (5, 6): Ch1, 6 (8, 10)sc. Join.

Round 5 (6, 7): Ch1, sc2tog 3 (4, 5) times. [3 (4, 5)sc]. Break yarn, leaving a 6in tail. Using a tapestry needle, sew the top of the mitten closed by weaving the yarn in and out of the last 3 (4, 5) stitches, pulling them tight to close. Tie off end.

Cloud (Makes 2)

Using yarn for the cloud and the smaller hook, ch4.

Round 1: 2sc in 2nd chain from hook, 1sc, 4sc in next ch, turning

your work to work in other side of chain, 1sc, 2sc in next ch. Join. [10sc].

Round 2: 6dc in the same st, [1slst, 6dc in the next st] twice, 1slst. [21 sts].

Using the photo for placement, sew onto the back of each mitten.

Sun

Using yarn for the sun and smaller hook, ch1 (does not count as a st), 6sc into a magic loop. Join. [6sc].

Round 1: Ch1 (does not count as a st), [2sc in next sc] six times. Join. [12sc].

Fasten off and weave in ends.

Using the photo for placement, sew onto the hand side of the mitten flap using a backstitch around the edge of the circle.

Rainbow

Using the photos for placement, embroider a rainbow onto one side of the mitten flap.

Finishing

To add the lines of rain and sun rays, thread your needle with the appropriate yarn and use running stitch to sew lines coming down from the cloud and rays coming out from the sun.

Using your button loop as a guide, sew on the button to the back of the mitten to keep the flap up.

GLASS SLIPPERS

Lacy and delicate, these quick slippers add
a touch of glamour to any little feet.

skill level: intermediate

Size	0-6 months	6-12 months	1 year	2 years
Width	2in	2⅛in	2⅛in	2⅛in
Length	3½in	4in	4¼in	5in
Yarn amounts	41yd	42yd	57yd	68yd

MATERIALS:
- 1¾oz skein of Malabrigo Silky Merino (51% silk, 49% merino wool), 138m Cape Cod Grey (429)
- F5/3.75mm hook
- 2 x buttons (½in in diameter)
- Tapestry needle
- 7½ (7¾, 8¼, 9¼)in of thin elastic cord or doubled shirring elastic tied or sewn into a loop

YARN REVIEW:
Silky and soft, this glamorous sport weight yarn is a joy to work with.

YARN ALTERNATIVES:
Fyberspates Scrumptious Silk DK

GAUGE:
Work 21sts and 23 rounds in single crochet to measure 4in square using F5/3.75mm hook, or size required to obtain gauge.

PATTERN NOTES:
- Do not count the ch1 at the beginning of the round as a stitch.
- Do not turn your work at the end of each round, unless indicated.

SPECIAL STITCHES:
Toe Gather
[YO twice, skip one stitch, insert hook in next stitch, YO and pull through stitch, (YO and pull through two loops) twice] six times (seven loops on hook), YO, pull through all the loops on hook.

INSTRUCTIONS:

Ch12 (13, 15, 17).

Round 1: 2sc in 2nd ch from hook, 9 (10, 12, 14)sc, 4sc in last st, turning as you go. Working in other side of the chain, 9 (10, 12, 14)sc, 2sc in first chain that has 2sc in it. Join. [26 (28, 32, 36)sc].

Round 2: Ch1, [2sc in sc] twice, 9 (10, 12, 14)sc, [2sc in next sc] four times, 9 (10, 12, 14)sc, [2sc in next sc] twice. Join. [34 (36, 40, 44)sc].

For size 0–6 months ONLY

Round 3: Ch1, 3sc, 2sc in next sc, 9 (-, -, -) sc, [2sc in next sc, 1sc] four times, 9 (-, -, -) sts, 2sc in next sc, 3sc. Join. [40 (-, -, -)sc].

For sizes 6–12 months, 1 year and 2 years ONLY

Round 3: Ch1, 3hdc, 2hdc in next sc, - (10, 12, 14)hdc, [2hdc in next sc, 1 hdc] four times, - (10, 12, 14)hdc, 2hdc in next sc, 3hdc. Join. [- (42, 46, 50)hdc].

For ALL sizes

Round 4: Ch1, 4sc, 2sc in next hdc, 4 (5, 6, 7)sc, 5 (5, 6, 7)hdc, 2hdc in next hdc, 5hdc, 2hdc in next, 4hdc, 2hdc in next hdc, 5 (5, 6, 7)hdc, 4 (5, 6, 7)sc, 2sc in next hdc, 4sc. Join. [45 (47, 51, 55) sts].

Round 5: Ch1, 5sc, 2sc in next sc, 4 (5, 6, 7) sc, 5 (5, 6, 7)hdc, 2hdc in next hdc, 13hdc, 2hdc in next hdc, 5 (5, 6, 7)hdc, 4 (5, 6, 7)sc, 2sc in next st, 5sc. Join. Turn. [49 (51, 55, 59) sts].

Uppers

With outside facing (RS), work 1 (1, 2, 2) rounds even in sc. Join.

Round 2 (2, 3, 3): Ch1, 16 (17, 19, 21) sc, [sc2tog, 1sc] six times, 15 (16, 18, 20) sc. Join. [43 (45, 49, 53)sc].

Work 1 (1, 2, 2) rounds even in sc. Join.

Round 4 (4, 6, 6): Ch2, 15 (16, 18, 20) 1hdc, ch2, work toe gather (see special stitches), ch2, sk one st, 15 (16, 18, 20) hdc. Join. [31 (33, 37, 41) sts].

Round 5 (5, 7, 7): Ch1, working over the elastic, 13 (14, 16, 18)sc, sc2tog, [1sc in ch] twice, 1sc, [1sc in ch] twice, sc2tog, 13 (14, 16, 18)sc. Join. [33 (35, 39, 43)sc].

Fastening

Slipper 1: Turn. 9 (10, 10, 11)slst, 20 (22, 24, 26)ch, 1slst in next st. Break yarn and weave in ends.

Slipper 2: 9 (10, 10, 11)slst, 20 (22, 24, 26)ch, 1slst in next st. Break yarn and weave in ends.

Sew on button on opposite side to ch loop, approximately two stitches back from the toe gather.

HEDGEHOG MITTENS

These little mittens are perhaps my favorite of all my designs
(just don't tell the others).

skill level: intermediate

Size	Small	Medium	Large
Hand circumference	4¾in	6in	7in
Hand length	5½in	6¼in	7in
Yarn amounts	79yd	119yd	167yd

MATERIALS:
- Main Color (MC): ⅞ (⅞, 1¾)oz of Jamieson's Shetland Spindrift, 4ply (100 % Shetland wool), 115yd/ball Moorit (108)
- Contrast Color (CC): ⅞oz of Jamieson's Shetland Spindrift, 4ply (100% Shetland wool), Mogit (107)
- D3/3.00mm hook
- C2/2.5mm hook
- Embroidery needle
- Small amount of black embroidery floss or thin black yarn for eyes and nose
- Stitch marker

YARN REVIEW:
This fingering yarn comes straight from the islands of Shetland; there are over 160 colors in the range and its lovely tweedy texture is perfect for this project.

YARN ALTERNATIVES:
Rowan Fine Tweed

GAUGE:
Work 24 sts and ten rounds in single crochet to measure 4in square using D3/3.00mm hook, or size required to obtain gauge.

SPECIAL STITCHES:
Bobble Stitch (BS)
[YO, insert hook into stitch, YO and pull through, YO and pull through two loops on the hook] four times. YO and pull through remaining five loops on the hook.

Pattern notes:

This pattern is worked entirely in the round in the amigurumi style, with no seams or turning chains at the start of the rounds. Use a stitch marker to mark the beginning of each round.

Do not turn your work at the end of each round.

INSTRUCTIONS:

With larger hook and CC, ch1,
6sc into a magic loop. [6sc].
Round 1: ★2sc in sc; rep from ★
around. [12sc].
Round 2: 12sc.
Round 3: ★1sc, 2sc in next sc; rep from
★ around. [18sc].
Round 4: 18dc.
Round 5: ★2sc, 2sc in next sc; rep from
★ around. [24sc].
Round 6: 24sc.

For Small size, break yarn and continue
to the Body section.

For sizes Medium and Large ONLY
Round 7: ★3sc, 2sc in next sc; rep from
★ around. [30sc].
Round 8: 30sc.

For Medium size, break yarn and
continue to the Body section.

For size Large ONLY
Round 9: ★4sc, 2sc in next sc; rep from
★ around. [36sc].
Round 10: 36sc.
Break yarn, continue to the Body
section.

Body
For ALL sizes
Tip: When working the odd number
rounds, move the stitch marker one
stitch to the left at the end of the round
to keep the BS in line with those of the
previous rounds.
Join MC.
Round 1: 24 (30, 36)sc.
Round 2: [1sc, 1BS] 6 (8, 9)
times, 1sc, 11 (13, 17)dc. [24 (30, 36) sts].
Rounds 3–8 (10, 12): Rep rounds
1–2. [24 (30, 36) sts].

For Left Mitten
Round 9 (11, 13): 13 (17, 19)sc, 6 (6,
7)ch, sk 4 (4, 5)sts, 7 (9, 12)sc. [20 (26,
31)sc].

For Right Mitten
Round 9 (11, 13): 19 (25, 30)sc, 6 (6,
7)ch, sk 4 (4, 5)sts, 1sc, [20 (26, 31)sc].

For Both Mittens
Round 10 (12, 14): [1sc, 1BS] 6
(8, 9) times, sc across, working
1sc in each ch from the previous
round. [26 (32, 38) sts].
Round 11 (13, 15): 26 (32, 38)sc.
Round 12 (14, 16): 26 (32, 38)dc.
Rounds 13 (15, 17) – 16 (18, 20):
Switch to the smaller hook, ★FPdc,
BPdc; rep from ★ to end. Break yarn and
weave in ends.

Thumb
Round 1: Re-attach MC yarn at the
first skipped stitch for the thumbhole.
Work sc around the thumb opening,
working in the skipped stitches and
then in the spaces between the dc
stitches on the other side of the thumb
opening. 10 (10, 12)sc.
Rounds 2–4 (4, 5): 10 (10, 12)sc.
Round 5 (5, 6): [3 (3, 4)sc, sc2tog]
twice. [8 (8, 10)sc].
Round 6 (6, 7): [2 (2, 3)sc, sc2tog]
twice. [6 (6, 8)sc].

For size Large ONLY
Round 8: [2sc, sc2tog] twice. [- (-, 6)sc].

For ALL sizes
Break yarn, leaving a 6in tail. Use the
tail and your tapestry needle to sew the
top of the thumb closed.
Thread your sewing needle with black
embroidery floss and, using the photo
as a guide, embroider eyes and nose
with a satin stitch.
Weave in ends.

LEG WARMERS

Whether you want to channel your inner *Flashdance* or simply keep the gap between trousers and socks warm, these legwarmers will do the job.

skill level: intermediate

Size	Newborn	Baby	Toddler	4+ years
Circumference	6in	7in	8in	9in
Length	7in	7½in	7¾in	9in
Yarn amounts	211yd	244yd	299yd	357yd

MATERIALS:
- 3½oz of Zitron Trekking XXL (75% superwash wool, 25% polyamide), 460yd/ball Oatmeal (215)
- D3/3.25mm hook
- F5/3.75mm hook
- Tapestry needle

YARN REVIEW:
This is a fingering weight wool, which when worked with a slightly larger hook than called for creates a warm and soft fabric.

YARN ALTERNATIVES:
Regia Tweed 4ply

GAUGE:
Work 10 sts and 10 rows in Crossed Puff Stitch pattern to measure 4in square using F5/3.75mm hook, or size required to obtain gauge.

SWATCH PATTERN
Ch33.

Row 1: Starting in the 7th ch from hook (counts as ch3 tch and 3 skipped sts), 1hdc, ch2, 1 Puff Stitch (PS) in the first skipped st, ★sk 2 sts, 1hdc in next st, ch2, 1PS in same st as the 1hdc from the previous st; rep from ★ to end. Join. Turn. [10 Crossed Puff Stitches].

Rows 2–10: Ch4, sk 2, 1hdc, ch2, 1PS in the same st as the slst join from the previous round, ★ sk 2 sts, 1hdc in next st, ch2, 1PS in same st as the 1hdc from the previous st; rep from ★ to end. Join. Turn. [10 Crossed Puff Stitches].

SPECIAL STITCHES

Puff Stitch (PS)

[YO, insert hook into stitch and draw up a loop] twice (five loops on hook). YO and pull through four loops on hook. YO and pull through last two loops on hook.

Crossed Puff Stitch (CPS)

First stitch: Ch2, sk 2 sts, 1hdc in next st, ch2, PS in bottom of ch2 before the 2 skipped stitches. [1 CPS].
Following stitches: Ch2, sk 2 sts, 1hdc in next stitch, ch2, 1PS in the same stitch as the previous hdc before the 2 skipped stitches. [1CPS].

INSTRUCTIONS (Make 2):
With the smaller hook, ch 46 (52, 60, 66). Join in the round.
Round 1: Ch3, 46 (52, 60, 66)dc. Join. [46 (52, 60, 66)dc].
Rounds 2–3: Ch3, *FPdc, BPdc; rep from * to end. Join. [46 (52, 60, 66) sts].
Round 4: Ch4, sk 3 (3, 2, 2) sts, 1hdc, ch2, 1PS in the same st as the slst join from the previous round, *sk 2 sts, 1hdc in next st, ch2, 1PS in same st as the 1hdc from the previous st; rep from * to end. Join. Turn. [15 (17, 20, 22)CPS].

Rounds 5–15 (16, 17, 20): Ch3, 15 (17, 20, 22)CPS. Join. Turn. [15 (17, 20, 22)CPS].
Round 16 (17, 18, 21): Ch3, 4dc, *3dc, sk one st; rep from * to end. Join. [46 (52, 60, 66)dc].
Rounds 17 (18, 19, 22) – 18 (19, 20, 23): Rep rounds 2–3.
Break yarn and weave in tails.

Pattern notes:
Do not count the ch3 at the beginning of the round as a stitch.
Do not turn the rounds when working the cuff ribbing.
Turn the rounds when working the CPS pattern.

MERMAID TAIL

New babies spend so very much of their time asleep.
A sweet little mermaid tail not only keeps them warm,
but makes for some adorable new baby photos.

MATERIALS:

- 8¾oz of Cascade Eco+ (100% Peruvian wool), 478yd/hank Pacific (2433)
- H8/5.00mm hook
- I9/5.50mm hook
- Tapestry needle
- 2 x buttons (1in in diameter)
- Stitch marker

YARN REVIEW:

This is a warm, bulky yarn, which makes this a quick project. The color has hints of silver, making it sparkle like the sea.

YARN ALTERNATIVES:

Wendy Mode Chunky

GAUGE:

14 sts and 13 rows in single crochet ribbing to measure 4in square using an H8/5mm hook, or size required to obtain gauge.

2.5 sts and 7 rows in shell stitch to measure 4in square using I9/5.5mm hook, or size required to obtain gauge.

SPECIAL STITCHES:

Shell Stitch (Sh)
Set-up row: Sk 2 sts, 5dc in next st, sk 2 sts, 1sc in next st.
Subsequent rows: 1sc in 3rd dc of shell, 5dc in sc.

Shell Decrease (Sh dec)

5dc in sc from previous round. Insert hook in the 3rd dc of the shell from the previous round, YO and draw up a loop. Insert hook in next sc, YO, draw up a loop, insert hook in 3rd dc of the next shell, YO and draw up a loop. YO and pull through all four loops on the hook.

PATTERN NOTES:

This sleep sack is as cute as can be, but is also practical. The waistband is worked first in ribbing, then the shell stitch is worked directly onto the ribbing, first in rows then joined in the round from the top down. A series of increases and decreases are made for the tail, before stitching it closed and constructing the fins.

skill level:
intermediate

Size	**0–6 months**
Finished waist	16–18in
Finished length	26in
Yarn amounts	327yd

INSTRUCTIONS:

Waistband

Using smaller hook, ch10. Turn at the end of each row.

Row 1(RS): Starting in 2nd chain from hook, 9sc. Turn. [9sc].

Rows 2–3: Ch1, 9sc in BLO. Turn. [9sc].

Row 4: Ch1, 1sc in BLO, ch2, sk 2 sts, 3sc in BLO, sk 2 sts, 1sc. Turn. [5sc].

Rows 5–6: Ch1, 9sc in BLO. Turn. [9sc].

Row 7: Rep Row 4.

Rows 8–64: Ch1, 9sc in BLO. Turn. [9 sc].

Tail set-up row: Without breaking the yarn, turn your work so you can work across the ribbing, RS facing. 54sc, working one stitch in the end of each row for 54 rows. Turn. [54sc].

Tail

Row 1: Using larger hook, ch1, 1sc, 9Sh, sk 2 sts, 1sc. Turn. [9Sh].

Row 2: Ch3 (counts as 1dc), 2dc in first sc, 9Sh 3dc in last sc. Turn. [9Sh].

Row 3: Ch1, 1sc, 9Sh. Turn. [9Sh].

Row 4: As Row 2. Do not turn.

You will now start working in rounds. Mark the start of the round with a stitch marker.

Round 1: Fold work in half and sc in the top of the first ch3 in the previous row. This will connect the work into the round. ★2Sh, [3dc, ch1, 1sc, ch1, 3dc] in same st; rep from ★ around. [9Sh].

Round 2: ★3Sh, place the sc from the 3rd Sh in second (centre) dc of the first dc cluster made, 5dc in the next sc, sc in second dc of the next dc cluster; rep from ★ around. [12Sh].

Rounds 3–21: Work even in established shell pattern, making 1sc in 3rd dc of the shell stitch from the previous round, 5dc in the next sc of the previous round.

Round 22: (1Sh dec, 4Sh) twice. [10Sh].

Rounds 23–24: Work even in established shell pattern.

Round 25: (3Sh,1Sh dec) twice. [8Sh].

Rounds 26–27: Work even in established shell pattern.

Round 28: (1Sh dec, 2Sh) twice. [6Sh].

Rounds 29–30: Work even in established shell pattern.

Round 31: (1Sh, 1Sh dec) twice. [4Sh].

Round 32: Work even in established shell pattern.

Finishing: Line up the tail so that the

slit at the waistband is just slightly off to one side. Flatten. Sc the tail closed at the bottom. Do not break yarn.

Fin

Work all sc stitches in the fin in BLO. Using larger hook, ch21.

Row 1: Starting with the 2nd chain from hook, 20sc back up to the tail. Join in the same stitch that the ch starts from. Turn. [20sc].

Row 2: Slst in next sc of tail (counts as tch), 18sc. Turn. [18sc].

Row 3: Ch1, 11sc, sc2tog, 5sc back up to tail. Join in the same st as slst. Turn. [17sc].

Row 4: Slst in next sc of tail (counts as tch), 5sc, sc2tog, 9sc. Turn. [15sc].

Row 5: Ch1, 9sc, sc2tog, 3sc back up to tail. Join in the same st as slst. Turn. [13sc].

Row 6: Slst in the next sc of the tail (counts as tch), 3sc, sc2tog, 8sc. Turn. [12sc].

Row 7: Ch1, 7sc, sc2tog, 3sc back up to tail. Join in the same st as slst. Break yarn. [11sc].

Join yarn at opposite side of end of tail. Rep Fin rows 1–7. Do not break yarn. Slst the two halves of the fin together. Break yarn and weave in tails.

Buttons

The buttons are sewn on approx. ½in away from the edge on the end of the ribbing that does not have buttonholes. Use the buttonholes for a guide on the placement. The two sets of buttonholes allow you to expand the waist of the sleep sack as the baby grows.

TUTU

There are certain wardrobe items that (sadly) children can pull off that adults can't. Tutus are on that list.

skill level: intermediate

Size	1 year	2 years	4 years	6 years
Finished waist	20¾in	21¼in	22in	22¾in
Finished length	6¼in	7in	10in	11in
Yarn amounts	531yd	554yd	729yd	780yd

MATERIALS:
- 10½ (10½, 14, 14)oz of Sirdar Snuggly Baby Bamboo DK (80% bamboo, 20% wool), 95m Flip Flop (125)
- 21¼ (21½, 22½, 23)cm of ¾in wide elastic webbing sewn securely in a loop for waist band.
- G6/4.00mm hook
- Tapestry needle
- Stitch marker

YARN REVIEW:
Baby Bamboo is one of my favorite yarns to use for babies and toddlers, as it's lovely to work with and washes extremely well. Combine this with the shimmer and luxury of bamboo and you have simply a lovely sport weight yarn.

YARN ALTERNATIVES:
Rowan Baby Silk Merino DK
Fyberspates Scrumptious DK

GAUGE:
Work 17 sts and 23 rows in single crochet to measure 4in square using a G6/4mm hook, or size required to obtain gauge.

Pattern notes:

Do not count the ch1 at the beginning of the round or row as a stitch.

Do not turn your work at the end of each round.

INSTRUCTIONS:

Ch90 (92, 94, 98). Join in the round.

Waistband

Rounds 1–17: Ch1, 90 (92, 94, 98)sc. Join. [90 (92, 94, 98)sc].

Round 18: Fold the waistband in half, long edges aligned, insert your elastic webbing in the opening. Working through all four loops, sc the waistband closed with the elastic inside.

Skirt

Round 19: (It may help to add a stitch marker here to find the back loops when you come back to work on the Drop underskirt.) Working in the FLO of the previous round, ch1, *1sc, 2sc in next sc; rep from * around. Join. [135 (138, 141, 147)sc].

Rounds 20–33 (36, 39, 42): Ch1, 1sc in each st around. Join. [135 (138, 141, 147)sc].

Drop Underskirt

Round 34 (37, 40, 43): Break yarn and re-attach in the back loops at the beginning of the round where you worked the skirt in the front loops. Working in BLO, ch1, 90 (92, 94, 98)sc. Join. [90 (92, 94, 98)sc].

Rounds 35 (38, 41, 44) – 39 (43, 47, 51): Ch1, 90 (92, 94, 98)sc. Join. [90 (92, 94, 98)sc].

Repeat rounds 19–39 (43, 47, 51) two (two, three, three) times.

Repeat rounds 19–33 (36, 39, 42) once. Break yarn. Weave in ends.

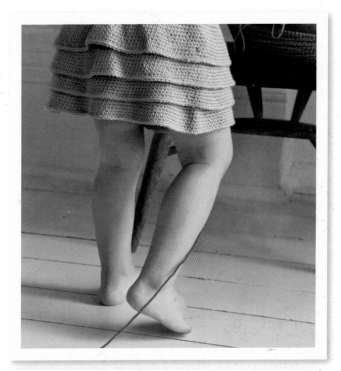

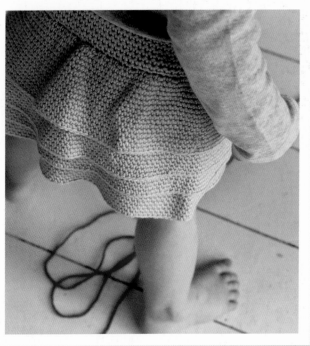

WHOLE
SELF

Cabled Yoke Cardigan
The Professor
Rainbow Bright
Silver Birch Tunic
Wolf

CABLED YOKE CARDIGAN

The swirling horizontal cable on this cardigan adds a touch of elegance and interest to a basic staple of a baby's wardrobe.

skill level: intermediate

Size	Newborn	0–6 months	6–12 months	1 year
Chest circumference	19in	19¾in	22in	23½in
Yarn amounts	218yd	237yd	305yd	349yd

MATERIALS:
- 3½ (5¼, 5¼, 7)oz of Sirdar Snuggly Baby Bamboo DK (80% bamboo, 20% wool), 95m Warm Grey (170)
- 6 (7, 7, 8) x buttons (approx. ¼in in diameter)
- G6/4.00mm hook
- Tapestry needle
- Sewing needle
- Thread

YARN REVIEW:
A blend of bamboo and wool, this lovely silky sport weight yarn is both elegant and washable—perfect for children's wear.

YARN ALTERNATIVES:
King Cole Bamboo Cotton DK
Sublime Baby Silk and Bamboo Yarn DK

GAUGE:
Work 17 sts and 23 rows in single crochet to measure 4in square using G6/4mm hook, or size required to obtain gauge.

Pattern note: The cable is worked first, with the decreases from the cable to the neck built on top and the chest and sleeves picked up around the bottom.

INSTRUCTIONS:

Cable

Ch10.

Row 1 (RS): Starting in the 4th ch from hook, 7dc. Turn. [8 sts].

Row 2: Ch3 (counts as a st), 6BPdc, 1dc. Turn. [8 sts].

Row 3: Ch3, sk 3 sts, 3FPtr, 3FPtr in the 3 skipped sts, 1dc in last st. Turn. [8 sts].

Row 4: Rep row 2.

Row 5: Ch3, 6FPdc, 1tr. Turn. [8 sts].

Work rows 2–5 18 (20, 21, 22) times.

Cable to Neck Decreases

Do not count the chain stitches at the beginning of the row as a stitch, unless indicated.

Turn your work, so you can work along the long edge, WS facing.

Row 1 (WS): Ch1, 1sc in the end of each row. Turn. [72 (80, 84, 88)sc].

Row 2: Ch1, 0 (2, 0, 4)sc, [10 (11, 12, 12)sc, sc2tog] six times. Turn. [66 (74, 78, 82)sc].

Row 3: Ch1, 0 (2, 0, 4)sc, [9 (10, 11, 11) sc, sc2tog] six times. Turn. [60 (68, 72, 76)sc].

Row 4: Ch1, 0 (2, 0, 4)sc, [8 (9, 10, 10)sc, sc2tog] six times. Turn. [54 (62, 66, 70)sc].

Row 5: Ch1, 0 (2, 0, 4)sc, [7 (8, 9, 9)sc, sc2tog] six times. Turn. [48 (56, 60, 64)sc].

Row 6: Ch1, 0 (2, 0, 4)sc, [6 (7, 8, 8)sc, sc2tog] six times. Turn. [42, (50, 54, 58)sc].

Row 7: Ch1, 0 (2, 0, 4)sc, [5 (6, 9, 9)sc, sc2tog] six times. Turn. [36 (44, 48, 52)sc].

For Newborn size, go to row 9.

For sizes 0–6 months, 6–12 months and 1 year ONLY

Row 8: Ch1, - (2, 0, 4)sc, [- (5, 8, 8)sc, sc2tog] six times. Turn. [- (38, 42, 46)sc].

For ALL sizes

Row 9: Ch2 (counts as 1 st), [sk 1 st, 1dc in next st, 1dc in skipped st] rep across 17 (18, 20, 22) times, 1dc in the last st. Turn. [36 (38, 42, 46)dc]. Break yarn. Turn your work and rejoin your yarn at the long edge of the bottom of the cable, WS facing.

Chest

Row 1 (WS): Ch1 (does not count as a st), working in the ends of each row [1sc, 2sc in the next] 36 (40, 42, 44) times. Turn. [108 (120, 126, 132)sc].

Row 2: Ch1, sc across, increase 10 (0, 6, 8) stitches evenly spaced across the row. Turn. [118 (120, 132, 140)sc].

Split the Body and Sleeves

Row 3: Ch1, 17 (17, 20, 21)sc, 6 (7, 8, 8) fsc, sk 24 (25, 26, 28), 36 (36, 40, 42)sc, 6 (7, 8, 8)fsc, sk 24 (25, 26, 28), 17 (17, 20, 21)sc. Turn. [82 (84, 96, 100)sts].

Rows 4–26 (28, 32, 34): Ch1, 82 (84, 96, 100)sc. Turn.

Edging

Row 1: Ch2, ★sk 1 sc, 1dc in next sc, 1dc in the skipped st; rep across 40 (41, 47, 49) times, 1dc in last st. [82 (84, 96, 100)dc].

Row 2: Ch1, 82 (84, 96, 100)sc. Turn.

Row 3: Rep Row 2

Row 4: Ch2, ★FPdc, BPdc; rep from ★ around.

Break yarn and weave in ends.

Sleeves (Make 2)

With RS facing, rejoin yarn in the middle of the fsc made for the armholes.

Round 1(RS): 24 (26, 34, 36): ch1, 30 (31, 34, 36)sc. Join. Turn. [30 (31, 34, 36) sc].

Sleeve Edging

Round 1: Ch2 (counts as 1 st), ★sk 1 sc, 1dc in next sc, 1dc in skipped st; rep 4 (15, 16, 17) times. For 0–6 months, 6–12 months and 1 year only: 1dc in last st. Turn. [30 (31, 34, 36)sc].

Round 2: Ch1, 30 (31, 34, 36)sc. Join. Turn.

Round 3: Ch2, 29 (30, 33, 35)dc. Join. Turn.

Round 4: Ch2 (counts as a st)★FPdc, BPdc; rep from ★ around.

Break yarn and weave in ends.

Buttonholes

For boys' garments, buttonholes are worked on the right side of the garment and girls' buttonholes are worked on the left.

Row 1: Join yarn at the front edge of the garment, RS facing on the side where you want to work the buttonholes. Make 1sc in the end of each sc row, 2sc in the end of each dc row and 1 st in each st in the cable section up to the neck. Turn. [48 (51, 55, 57)sc].

Row 2 (WS): Ch1, 3 (1, 3, 1)sc, ★ch1, sk 1 st, 5sc; rep from around 6 (7, 7, 8) times, 2 (1, 3, 1)sc. [42 (44, 48, 49)sc]. Break yarn and weave in ends.

Buttonband

Row 1: Join yarn at the front edge of the garment, on the opposite side to where you are working your buttonholes. Make 1sc in the end of each sc row, 2sc in the end of each dc row and 1 st in each st in the cable section up to the neck. Turn. [48 (51, 55, 57)sc].

Row 2: Ch1, 41 (44, 48, 50)sc. Break yarn and weave in ends. Using the buttonholes as a guide, sew buttons securely in place using sewing needle and thread.

THE PROFESSOR

Vests with cables and shawl collars are one of my favorite garments to make and wear. I love the way they accentuate the little old man factor in babies, while also being practical, keeping their core bodies and little necks warm.

skill level: intermediate

Size	0–6 months	6–12 months	1 year	2 years	4 years	6 years
Finished chest	18½in	20½in	21¼in	22½in	25½in	27¼in
Finished length	9½in	10¼in	11in	11¾in	12½in	14in
Yarn amounts	308yd	371yd	442yd	494yd	544yd	669yd

MATERIALS:
- 5¼ (5¼, 7, 7, 8¾, 10½)oz Extra Fine Merino Wool DK (100% merino wool), 127yd/ball Mocha (020)
- G6/4.00mm hook
- 4 x buttons (1in in diameter)
- Tapestry needle

YARN REVIEW:
Sumptuous, with great stitch definition, this sport weight superwash merino is the perfect mix of luxury and wearability.

YARN ALTERNATIVES:
Wendy Merino DK
MillaMia Naturally Soft Merino

GAUGE:
20 sts and 14 rows in basket weave (see special stitches) to measure 4in square using G6/4.00mm hook, or size required to obtain gauge.
20 sts and 20 rows in single crochet ribbing (see special stitches) to measure 4in square using G6/4.00mm hook, or size required to obtain gauge.

SPECIAL STITCHES:

Basket Weave

Basket weave stitch is created by alternating sets of FPdc and BPdc stitches in groups of four to create stitches that pop out or recede on alternate sides of the fabric. After four rows of raising the stitches on one side, alternate the direction of the raised stitches to push the stitches out on the other side of the garment.

For multiples of eight stitches:

Row 1: *4FPdc, 4BPdc; rep from * across. Turn.

Row 2: *4BPdc, 4FPdc; rep from * across. Turn.

Row 3: Rep row 1.

Row 4: Rep row 2.

Row 5: Rep row 2.

Row 6: Rep row 1.

Row 7: Rep row 2.

Row 8: Rep row 1.

Rep rows 1–8.

Single Crochet Ribbing

Rows of sc are worked into the BLO.

PATTERN NOTES:

• You will maintain the stitch pattern throughout.

• Do not count the chains at the beginning of the row as a stitch.

INSTRUCTIONS:

Ch 50 (54, 58, 62, 66, 74).

Row 1 (WS): Starting in the 3rd ch from hook, 48 (52, 56, 60, 64, 72)dc. Turn. [48 (52, 56, 60, 64, 72)sts].

Rows 2–5 (5, 7, 7, 7, 9): Ch2, work in basket weave pattern. Turn. [48 (52, 56, 60, 64, 72)sts].

Rows 6 (6, 8, 8, 8, 10) – 13 (13, 15, 15, 17, 19): Ch2, 28 (32, 36, 36, 40, 44) stitches in basket weave pattern. Turn. [28 (32, 36, 36, 40, 44)sts].

Row 14 (14, 16, 16, 18, 20): Ch2, 28 (32, 36, 36, 40, 44) stitches in basket weave pattern. 22 (22, 22, 26, 26, 30)ch. Turn. [28 (32, 36, 36, 40, 44) sts].

Row 15 (15, 17, 17, 19, 21): Starting in 3rd ch from hook, work 20 (20, 20, 24, 24, 28)dc in the chain, continue in basket weave pattern. Turn. [48 (52, 56, 60, 64, 72) sts].

Rows 16 (16, 18, 18, 20, 22) – 19 (19, 23, 23, 25, 29): Ch2, work in basket weave pattern. Turn. [48 (52, 56, 60, 64, 72)sts].

Row 20 (20, 24, 24, 26, 30): 4slst, ch2, work in basket weave pattern. Turn. [44 (48, 52, 56, 60, 68)sts].

Rows 21 (21, 25, 25, 27, 31) – 31 (35, 37, 39, 43, 47): Ch2, work in basket weave pattern. Turn. [44 (48, 52, 56, 60, 68)sts].

Row 32 (36, 38, 40, 44, 48): Ch2, work in basket weave pattern. 6ch. [44 (48, 52, 56, 60, 68) sts].

Row 33 (37, 39, 41, 45, 49): Starting in 3rd ch from hook, work 4hdc in the chain, continue in basket weave pattern. Turn. [48 (52, 56, 60, 64, 72)sts].

Rows 34 (38, 40, 42, 46, 50) – 37 (41, 45, 47, 51, 57): Ch2, work in basket weave pattern. Turn. [48 (52, 56, 60, 64, 72) sts].

Rows 38 (42, 46, 48, 52, 58) – 45 (49, 53, 55, 61, 67): Ch2, 28 (32, 36, 36, 40, 44) stitches in basket weave pattern. Turn. [28 (32, 36, 36, 40, 44) sts].

Row 46 (50, 54, 56, 62, 68): Ch2, 28 (32, 36, 36, 40, 44) stitches in basket weave pattern. 22 (22, 22, 26, 26, 30)ch. Turn. [28 (32, 36, 36, 40, 44) sts].

Row 47 (51, 55, 57, 63, 69): Starting in 3rd ch from hook, work 20 (20, 20, 24, 24, 28)dc in the chain, continue in basket weave pattern. Turn. [48 (52, 56, 60, 64, 72) sts].

Rows 48 (52, 56, 58, 64, 70) – 51 (55, 61, 63, 69, 77): Ch2, work in basket weave pattern. Turn. [48 (52, 56, 60, 64, 72) sts].

Break yarn and weave in ends.

Sewing Up

Lay the finished piece flat, with RS up (the original chained edge to the right, shoulders up). Fold the outer edges in, so that the shoulder "straps" line up. Dc the seams closed, weave in ends. Turn garment right side out.

Shawl Edge Ribbing

Rejoin yarn at the bottom front corner of garment (on the edge with the original chain, if you are making for a girl and on the final row if you are making for a boy). Work 1sc in the end of each row up the sides of the vest and around the neckline to create an even base for the ribbing.

[121 (131, 139, 149, 157, 173)sc].
Ch17 (19, 21, 25, 23, 27).

Row 1: Starting with the 2nd chain
from the hook, 16 (18, 20, 24, 22, 26)sc,
1slst in first sc of the sc edging on
the lapel. Turn. [16 (18, 20, 24, 22, 26)sc].

Row 2: 1slst in next sc on lapel (counts
as tch). 16 (18, 20, 24, 22, 26)sc BLO.
Turn. [16 (18, 20, 24, 22, 26)sc].

Row 3: Ch1, 16 (18, 20, 24, 22, 26)sc
BLO . Slst in first sc of the sc edging
on the lapel. Turn. [16 (18, 20, 24, 22, 26)
sc].

**Rows 4–121 (131, 139, 149, 157,
173):** Rep rows 2–3. Work buttonhole
on rows 6 (8, 8, 8, 10, 10) and 18 (20, 20,
20, 22, 22) as follows:

Slst in next sc on the lapel (counts as
tch). 3 (4, 4, 6, 5, 6)sc BLO, ch3, sk 3,
(4, 6, 6, 6, 8)sc BLO, ch3, sk 3sts, (4, 4, 6,
5, 6) sc in BLO. Turn. [10 (12, 14, 18, 16,
20)sts].

Break yarn and weave in ends.

RAINBOW BRIGHT

This quick and fun little dress makes a bold statement with its geometric shapes and bright colors. It is sized in a way that means that it can start as a dress and become a top as the child grows.

skill level: intermediate

Size	0-6 months	6-12 months	1 year	2 years	4 years	6 years
Finished chest	20½	22in	23¼in	24in	26¾	29in
Finished length	12½in	13in	13½in	14in	15in	16in
Yarn amounts	253yd	288yd	326yd	354yd	421yd	467yd

MATERIALS:
- Main Color (MC): 5¼ (7, 7, 7, 8¾, 10⅓)oz of Rico Creative Cotton Aran (100% cotton), 93yd/ball Mouse (28)
- 1¾oz of Rico Creative Cotton Aran (100% cotton) 93yd/ball in each of the following colors

- Color A: Red (05)
- Color B: Orange (74)
- Color C: Banana (63)
- Color D: Green (49)
- Color E: Royal (39)

- H8/5.00mm hook
- G6/4.5mm hook
- Stitch marker
- Tapestry needle

YARN REVIEW:
The colors in this range of affordable cotton yarn are so vibrant, it is hard to pick just one...

YARN ALTERNATIVES:
Knit Picks Simply Cotton Worsted Yarn

GAUGE:
8.25 sts and 16 rows in tweed stitch to measure 4in square using a G6/5mm hook, or size required to obtain gauge.

SPECIAL STITCHES:
Tweed Stitch
Set-up round: Ch1, ★1sc, ch1, sk 1 st; rep from ★ across.
All other rounds: Ch1, ★1sc in chsp, ch1; rep from ★ across.

PATTERN NOTES:
• Do not count the chains at the beginning of the round as a stitch.
• Do not turn your work at the end of each round.

INSTRUCTIONS:
Yoke
Using the larger hook, ch56 (60, 64, 68, 72, 76). Join in the round with a slst.
Row 1: Ch2, 56 (60, 64, 68, 72, 76)hdc. Join.
Row 2: Ch2, [3hdc, 2hdc in next hdc] 14 (15, 16, 17, 18, 19) times. Join. [70 (75, 80, 85, 90, 95)hdc].
Row 3: Ch2, 70 (75, 80, 85, 90, 95)hdc. Join.

Row 4: Ch2, [4hdc, 2hdc in next hdc] 14 (15, 16, 17, 18, 19) times. Join. [84 (90, 96, 102, 108, 114)hdc].

For sizes 0–6 months and 6–12 months ONLY go to round 1 of the Bodice.

For sizes 1 year, 2 years, 4 years and 6 years ONLY
Row 5: Ch2, - (-, -, 96, 102, 108, 114)hdc. Join.

For sizes 1 year and 2 years ONLY, go to Round 1 of the Bodice.

For sizes 4 years and 6 years ONLY
Row 6: Ch2, [5hdc, 2hdc in next hdc] - (-, -, -, 18, 18) times. - (-, -, -, 0, 6)hdc. Join. [- (-, -, -, 126, 132)hdc].

Bodice
Round 1 (this round is worked in BLO): Continuing in MC, ch1, [1sc, ch1, sk 1 st] 14 (15, 16, 17, 21, 22) times, 12 (14, 14, 14, 12, 14)fsc, sk 14 (15, 16, 17, 21, 22)sts, [1sc, ch1, sk 1 st] 14 (15, 16, 17, 21, 22) times, 12 (14, 14, 14, 12, 14)fsc, sk 14 (15, 16, 17, 21, 22). Join in the round. Break yarn. [52 (58, 60, 62, 66, 72)sc].
Round 2: Join Color A and mark beginning of round with a stitch marker, ch1, [1sc, ch1, sk 1 st] 6 (7, 7, 7, 6, 7) times, [1sc in chsp, ch1] 14 (15, 16, 17, 21, 22) times, [1sc, ch1, sk 1 st] 6 (7, 7, 7, 6, 7) times, [1sc in chsp, ch1] 14 (15, 16, 17, 21, 22) times. Join. Break yarn. [40 (44, 46, 48, 54, 58)sc].

Round 3: Switch to MC, Ch1, [1sc, ch1, 1sc] in the same chsp, ch1, [1sc in chsp, ch1] 20 (22, 23, 24, 27, 29) times, [1sc, ch1, 1sc] in same chsp, ch1, [1sc in chsp, ch1] 20 (22, 23, 24, 27, 29) times. Join. Break yarn. [42 (46, 48, 50, 56, 60)sc].
Round 4: Switch to Color B: Ch1, work in tweed stitch around. Join. Break yarn. [42 (46, 48, 50, 56, 60)sc].
Rounds 5–43 (45, 47, 49, 51, 53): Rep round 4, changing the colors in pattern. The color pattern in this section is worked as follows:
Round 5: MC
Round 6: Color C
Round 7: MC
Round 8: Color D
Round 9: MC
Round 10: Color E
Round 11: MC
Round 12: Color A
Round 13: MC
Round 14: Color B
Repeat as required.
Rounds 44 (46, 48, 50, 52, 54) – 47 (49, 52, 54, 57, 59): Switch to the smaller hook, ch2, working 1hdc in each ch sp and each sc, 84 (92, 96, 100, 112, 120) hdc. Join.
Break yarn and weave in ends.

SILVER BIRCH TUNIC

Inspired by the forests of Scotland in spring, this yoke-necked tunic dress can be made in a variety of ways to suit the seasons. The stitch pattern on the sleeves and dress reminds me of the dappled light coming through the branches of a tree.

skill level: intermediate

Size	3 months	6 months	1 year	2 years	4 years	6 years
Finished chest	19in	20in	20¾in	22in	24¼in	27in
Finished length	12in	13in	13½in	14½in	15¼in	16½in
Yarn amounts: Yoke	99yd	115yd	137yd	153yd	186yd	213yd
Yarn amounts: Bodice	301yd	372yd	399yd	454yd	558yd	679yd

MATERIALS:

For a Solid Color Dress

- 7 (7, 7, 10½, 10½, 14)oz Yarn Love Amy March (100% superwash merino), 270yd/hank Earl Grey

For a Multi-colored Dress

- Yoke: 3 ½oz Yarn Love Amy March (100% superwash merino), 270yd/hank Bouquet
- Bodice and Sleeves: 10½ (10½, 10½, 14, 17½)oz Rowan Pure Wool DK (100% superwash wool), 137yd/ball Earth (018)
- 2 x buttons (1in in diameter)
- Tapestry needle
- G6/4.00mm hook

YARN REVIEW:

A beautiful hand-dyed yarn, this sport weight superwash merino is a beautiful option for a full dress, or adds a bit of luxury at the yoke to a dress made out of a more commercially available wool.

YARN ALTERNATIVES:

King Cole Merino Blend DK
Patons Merino DK

GAUGE:

Work 17.5 sts and 20.5 rows in single crochet ribbing (through the back loop) to measure 4in square using G6/4mm hook, or size required to obtain gauge.

Work 7.5 sts and 15.5 rows in Angled Crochet to measure 4in square using G6/4mm hook, or size required to obtain gauge.

SPECIAL STITCHES:

Angled Crochet (AC)

Work (sc, ch2, sc) in the ch2 space from the previous row.

Angled Crochet Increase

(sc, ch2, sc, sc, ch2, sc) in the ch2 space from the previous row. 1 angled crochet stitch increased.

Pattern notes:

This pattern is worked from the top down from the yoke. Sleeves are crocheted on after the bodice is done. There are no seams. To ensure a nicely rounded yoke scatter the increase stitches rather than line them up.

INSTRUCTIONS:

Yoke

In this section, do not count the ch1 at the beginning of the row as a stitch. Using the yarn for the yoke, ch44 (48, 49, 51, 55, 59). Turn.

Row 1(RS): Starting in the 2nd ch from hook, 43 (47, 48, 50, 54, 58)sc. Turn. [43 (47, 48, 50, 54, 58)sc].

Rows 2–4: Ch1, work in BLO, sc across, increase by 5 (5, 4, 4, 4, 4 sts) evenly across the row. (Increase by working 2sc in sc.) Turn. [58 (62, 60, 62, 66, 70)sc].

Row 5: Ch1, work in BLO , 1sc, ch2, sk 2 sts, sc across, increase by 5 (5, 4, 4, 4, 4 sts) evenly across the row. Turn. [61 (65, 62, 64, 68, 72)s]c.

Row 6: Ch1, work in BLO, sc across to skipped sts, increase by 5 (5, 4, 4, 4, 4 sts) evenly across the row, 2sc in chsp, 1sc. Turn. [68 (72, 68, 70, 74, 78)sc].

Rows 7–12: As row 2. [98 (102, 92, 94, 98, 102)sc].

For sizes 3 months and 6 months ONLY

Row 13: As row 5. [101 (105, -, -, -, -)sc].

Row 14: As row 6. [108, (112, -, -, -, -)sc].

Rows 15–16: As row 2. [118 (122, -, -, -, -)sc].

For size 3 months ONLY

Break yarn and weave in ends.

For size 6 months ONLY

Rows 17–18: As row 2. [- (132, - , -, -, -)sc].

Break yarn and weave in ends.

For sizes 1 year and 2 years ONLY

Rows 13–16: As row 2. [- (-, 108, 110, -, -)sc].

Row 17: As row 5. [- (-, 110, 112, -, -)sc].

Row 18: As row 6.[- (-, 116, 118, -, -)sc].

Rows 19–23: As row 2.[- (-, 136, 138, -, -)sc].

For size 1 year ONLY
Break yarn and weave in ends.

For size 2 years ONLY
Row 24: As row 2. [- (-, -, -, 142, -, -)sc].
Break yarn and weave in ends.

For size 4 years and 6 years ONLY
Rows 13–20: As row 2. [- (-, -, -, 130, 134)sc].
Row 21: As row 5 [- (-, -, -, 132, 136)sc].
Row 22: As row 6. [- (-, -, -, 138, 142)sc].
Rows 23–26: As row 2. [- (-, -, -, 154, 158)sc].

For size 4 years ONLY
Break yarn and weave in ends.

For size 6 years ONLY
Rows 27–28: As row 2. [- (-, -, -, -, 166) sc].
Break yarn and weave in ends.

Bodice
Do not turn your work at the end of each round.
Join yarn for bodice and sleeves on the long edge at the bottom of the yoke, with RS side facing 13 (15, 15, 17, 17, 19) stitches in from the edge with the buttonholes.

Set-up for 3 months ONLY
Round 1: (Working in BLO) ch1 (does not count as a st), [1sc, ch2, 1sc, sk 1 st, 1sc, ch2, 1sc] seven times. 8fsc, sk 22 sts, [1sc, ch2, 1sc, sk 1, 1sc, ch2, 1sc] seven times. 8fsc. Skipping the remaining 13 stitches from the yoke, join with a slst in the ch2 space at the beginning of round. [72 sts].

Round 2: Ch3 (counts as 1sc and ch2), sc in same chsp, 13AC, [1sc, ch2, 1sc] four times across the fsc of the previous round, 14AC, [1sc, ch2, 1sc] four times across the fsc of the previous round. Join with a slst in the ch2 space at the beginning of round. [36 AC].

Set-up for 6 months ONLY
Round 1: (Working in BLO) Ch3 (counts as 1sc and ch2), 1sc, [1sc, ch2, 1sc, sk 1 st, 1sc, ch2, 1sc] seven times, 1sc, ch2, 1sc, 6fsc, sk 25 sts, 1sc, ch2, 1sc, [1sc, ch2, 1sc, sk 1 st, 1sc, ch2, 1sc] seven times, 1sc, ch2, 1sc, 6fsc, sk rem 15 stitches from yoke, join with a slst in the ch2 space at beginning of round. [76 sts].

Round 2: Ch3 (counts as 1sc and ch2), 1sc in same chsp, 15AC, [1sc, ch2, 1sc] three times across the fsc of the previous round, 16AC, [1sc, ch2, 1sc] three times across the fsc of the previous round. Join with a slst in the ch2 sp at beginning of round. [38 AC].

Set-up for 1 year ONLY
Round 1: (Working in BLO) ch1 (does not count as a st), [1sc, ch2, 1sc, sk 1 st, 1sc, ch2, 1sc] eight times. 8fsc, sk 26 sts, [1sc, ch2, 1sc, sk 1, 1sc, ch2, 1sc] eight times. 8fsc, sk rem 15 sts from yoke, join with a slst in the ch2 space at beginning of round. [80 sts].

Round 2: Ch3 (counts as 1sc and ch2), 1sc in same chsp, 15AC, [1sc, ch2, 1sc] four times across the fsc of the previous round, 16AC, [1sc, ch2, 1sc] four times across the fsc of the prev round. Join with a slst in ch2 sp at beginning of round. [40 AC].

Set-up for 2 years ONLY
Round 1: (working in BLO) Ch3 (counts as 1sc and ch2), 1sc, [1sc, ch2, 1sc, sk 1 st, 1sc, ch2, 1sc] eight times. 8fsc, sk 27 sts, 1sc, ch2, 1sc, [1sc, ch2, 1sc, sk 1, 1sc, ch2, 1sc] eight times. 8fsc. sk rem 15 stitches from yoke, join with a slst in ch2sp at beginning of round. [84 st].

Round 2: Ch3 (counts as 1sc and ch2), 1sc in same chsp, 16AC, [1sc, ch2, 1sc] four times across the fsc of the previous round, 17AC, [1sc, ch2, 1sc] four times across the fsc of the prev round. Join with a slst in the ch2 sp at beginning of round. [42 AC].

Set-up for 4 years ONLY
Round 1: (Working in BLO) ch1 (does not count as a st), [1sc, ch2, 1sc, sk 1 st, 1sc, ch2, 1sc] nine times. 10fsc, sk 30 sts, [1sc, ch2, 1sc, sk 1, 1sc, ch2, 1sc] nine times, 10fsc, sk rem 17 stitches from yoke, join with a slst in ch2 space at beginning of round. [92 sts].

Round 2: Ch3 (counts as 1sc and ch2), 1sc in same chsp, 17AC, [1sc, ch2, 1sc] five times across the fsc of the prev round, 18AC, [1sc, ch2, 1sc] five times across the fsc of the previous round. Join with a slst in the ch2 sp at beginning of round. [46AC].

Set-up for 6 years ONLY
Round 1: (Working in BLO) ch3 (counts as 1sc and ch2), 1sc [1sc, ch2, 1sc, sk 1, 1sc, ch2, 1sc] nine times, 1sc, ch2, 1sc, 10fsc, sk 32 sts, 1sc, ch2, 1sc [1sc, ch2, 1sc, sk 1 st, 1sc, ch2, 1sc] nine times, 1sc, ch2, 1sc, 10fsc, sk rem 18

sts from yoke, join with a slst in the ch2 sp at beg of round. [100 sts].

Round 2: Ch3 (counts as 1sc and ch2), sc in same chsp, 19AC, [1sc, ch2, 1sc] five times across the fsc of prev round, 20AC, [1sc, ch2, 1sc] five times. Join with a slst in the ch2sp at beginning of round. [50AC].

For ALL sizes

Rounds 3–7: (Ch3 (counts as 1sc and ch2), 1sc) in same chsp. Continue working AC in each ch2 space. Join with a slst in first ch2 space of round. [36 (38, 40, 42, 46, 50)AC].

Round 8: Complete 3 angled crochet increases spaced evenly across the round. [39 (41, 43, 45, 49, 53)AC].

Rounds 9–15: Continue working even in established pattern. [39 (41, 43, 45, 49, 53)AC].

Round 16: Complete 3 angled crochet increases spaced evenly across the round. [42 (44, 46, 48, 52, 56)AC].

Rounds 17–23: Continue working even [in established pattern. [42 (44, 46, 48, 52, 56)AC].

Round 24: Complete 3 angled crochet increases spaced evenly across the round. [45 (47, 49, 51, 55, 59)AC].

Rounds 25–31: Continue working even in established pattern. [45 (47, 49, 51, 55, 59)AC].

Round 32: Complete 3 angled crochet increases spaced evenly across the round. [48 (50, 52, 54, 58, 62)AC].

For sizes 3 months, 6 months and 1 year ONLY

Rounds 33–34 (37, 37): Continue working even in established pattern. Break yarn and weave in ends [48 (50, 52, -, -, -)AC].

For sizes 2 years, 4 years and 6 years ONLY

Rounds 33–39: Continue working even in established pattern. [- (-, -, 54, 58, 62) AC].

Round 40: Complete 3 angled crochet increases spaced evenly across the round. [- (-, -, 57, 61, 65)A]C.

For size 2 years ONLY

Round 41: Continue working even in established pattern. Break yarn and weave in ends. [- (-, -, 57, -, -)AC].

For sizes 4 years and 6 years ONLY

Rounds 41–42 (45): Work even for specified number of rows. Break yarn and weave in ends. [- (-, -, -, 61, 65)AC].

Sleeves

Do not turn your work at the end of each round.

When you work around the yoke section of the sleeves, you will work in the BLO. For the sleeve with the buttonholes, you will overlap 4 (5, 4, 5, 4, 5) stitches from each side, with the buttonholes on top. Pin them in place and work the top layer through the BLO. The underside should be worked through both loops to maintain the line of the stitches and also strengthen the seam.

Set-up for 3 months

Round 1: Join the yarn on the middle of the underarm created by the foundation sc, ch3 (counts as 1sc and ch2), 1sc, sk 1 st, 1sc, ch2, 1sc, [1sc, ch2, 1sc, sk 1 st, 1sc, ch2, 1sc] five times. Join with a slst in the ch2 space at the beginning of round. [12 AC].

Set-up for size 6 months ONLY

Round 1: Join yarn on the middle of the underarm created by the foundation sc, ch3 (counts as 1sc and ch2), 1sc, sk 1 st, [1sc, ch2, 1sc] six times, sk 1 st, [1sc, ch2, 1sc] six times, sk 1 st, 1sc, ch2, 1sc. Join with a slst in ch2 sp at beginning of round. [14AC].

Set-up for size 1 year ONLY

Round 1: Join yarn on the middle of the underarm created by the foundation sc, ch3 (counts as 1sc and ch2), 2sc, ch2, 1sc, [1sc, ch2, 1sc, sk 1 st, 1sc, ch2, 1sc] six times. Join with a slst in the ch2 space at beginning of round. [14 AC].

Set-up for size 2 years ONLY

Round 1: Join yarn on the middle of the underarm created by the foundation sc, ch3 (counts as 1sc and ch2), 2sc, ch2, 1sc, [1sc, ch2, 1sc, sk 1 st, 1sc, ch2, 1sc] five times. 1sc, ch2, 2sc, ch2, 2sc, ch2, 1sc. Join with a slst in the ch2 sp at beginning of round. [15 AC].

Set-up for size 4 years ONLY

Round 1: Join yarn on the middle of the underarm created by the foundation sc, ch3 (counts as 1sc and ch2), 2sc, ch2, 1sc, [1sc, ch2, 1sc, sk 1 st, 1sc, ch2, 1sc] seven times, sk 1 st. Join with a slst in ch2 sp at beginning of round. [16 AC].

Set-up for size 6 years ONLY

Round 1: Join yarn on the middle of the underarm created by the foundation sc. Ch3 (counts as 1sc and ch2), 1sc [1sc, ch2, 1sc] two times, [1sc, ch2, 1sc, sk 1 st, 1sc, ch2, 1sc] three times, [1sc, ch2, 1sc] three times, [1sc, ch2, 1sc, sk 1 st, 1sc, ch2, 1sc] three times. Join with a slst in ch2 sp at beginning of round. [18 AC].

For ALL sizes

Rounds 2–23 (27, 29, 33, 41, 48): Ch3 (counts as sc and ch2), sc in same ch2 space. Work AC in each ch2sp. [12 (14, 14, 15, 16, 18)AC].

Fasten off. Using the buttonholes as a guide, sew your buttons onto the appropriate side of the collar. Weave in yarn ends.

WOLF

Cable and ears take a normal hooded jumper and turn it into something rustic. The stodgy half treble stitches are worked in a way that creates a very solid and very warm fabric to keep little beasts snuggly on cold days. It is very generously sized to work over layers and last through growth spurts.

skill level: intermediate

Size	3 months	6 months	1 year	2 years	4 years	6 years
Finished chest	21¼	22in	26¼in	27¾in	29½in	30¾in
Finished length	13½in	15in	15¼in	16in	17½in	19in
Sleeve length	6¼in	7in	7½in	8¾in	10½in	12½in
Yarn amounts	437yd	567yd	681yd	780yd	948yd	1019yd

MATERIALS:
- 7, (8¾, 10½, 12¼, 14, 15¾)oz of Artesano Superwash Merino (100% superwash merino), 123yd/ball Grey (SFN41)
- G6/4.00mm hook
- Tapestry needle
- 7 (7, 8, 8, 9, 9) toggle-style buttons (approx. 1¼in long)

YARN REVIEW:
A fantastically soft sport weight superwash merino, this lovely yarn works up quickly with G6/4mm hook.

YARN ALTERNATIVES:
King Cole Merino Blend DK
Madelinetosh Tosh DK

GAUGE:
Work 13 sts and 13 rows in solid half double crochet (see special stitches) to measure 4in square using G6/4mm hook, or size required to obtain gauge.

SPECIAL STITCHES:

Solid Half Double (shdc)

All of the hdc stitches in the pattern are worked in the space between the stitches of the previous row. This creates a more solid, warm fabric and lessens the characteristic striping of crocheting in rows.

Solid Half Treble 2 Together (shdc2tog)

[YO, insert hook in the next space between the stitches, YO and pull through stitch] twice (five loops on hook), YO and pull through all the loops on the hook. One shdc decreased.

Foundation Half Double Crochet (fhdc)

Ch3, YO, insert hook in 3rd ch from hook, YO and pull through (three loops on hook), YO and pull through one loop (ch1 made), YO, and draw through all three loops on hook ★YO, insert hook in ch made in the last stitch, YO and pull through one loop (ch1 made), YO and pull through all three loops on hook; rep from ★ until you have required number of stitches.

Cable Pattern for Front and Hood

(Worked over ten stitches)

Cable Row 1 (RS): 2RhdcF, 1hdc, 4FPdtr in the stitches 2 rows below, 1hdc, 2FPhdc.

Cable Row 2 (WS): 2BPhdc, 6hdc, 2BPhdc.

Cable Row 3: 2FPhdc, 1hdc, sk 2 sts, [1FPdtr in FPdtr 2 rows below] twice 1FPdtr in first skipped FPdtr 2 rows below, 1FPdtr in next skipped FPdtr 2 rows below, 1hdc, 1FPhdc.

Cable Row 4: Rep row 2.

Cable Rows 5–6: Rep rows 1–2.

PATTERN NOTES:

• The cardigan is mostly seamless, worked from the top of the hood down.

• Instructions are available for boy (buttons on right) and girl (buttons on left) versions.

INSTRUCTIONS:

Hood (All Sizes)

Fhdc12.

Set-up Row (WS): Ch2 (counts as 1hdc), 10hdc, 4hdc in the last stitch turning as you go to work in the other side of the fhdc, 11hdc. Turn. [26 sts].

Row 1(RS): Ch2, work Row 1 of the Cable Pattern (working the FPdtr stitches in the fhdc of the foundation) [2hdc in hdc (worked in the stitch as normal, not the space as in shdc)] four times, work Row 1 of the Cable Pattern (working the FPdtr sts in the fhdc of the foundation) 1hdc. Turn. [30 sts].

Row 2: Ch2, work Row 2 of the Cable Pattern, [2hdc in hdc, 1shdc] four times, work Row 2 of the Cable Pattern, 1hdc. Turn. [34 sts].

Row 3: Ch2, work Row 3 of the Cable Pattern, [2shdc, 2hdc in hdc] four times, work Row 3 of the Cable Pattern, 1hdc. Turn. [38 sts].

Row 4: Ch2, work Row 4 of the Cable Pattern, [2hdc in hdc, 3shdc] four times, work Row 4 of the Cable Pattern, 1hdc. Turn. [42 sts].

Row 5: Ch2, work Row 5 of the Cable Pattern, [4shdc, 2hdc in hdc] four times, work Row 5 of the Cable Pattern, 1hdc. Turn. [46 sts].

Row 6: Ch2, work Row 6 of the Cable Pattern, [2hdc in hdc, 5shdc] four times, work Row 6 of the Cable Pattern, 1hdc. Turn. [50 (50, 50, 50, 50, 50) sts].

For size 3 months ONLY, go to row 12.

For sizes 6 months, 1 year, 2 years, 4 years, and 6 years ONLY

Row 7: Ch2, work Cable Pattern in established pattern, [6shdc, 2hdc in hdc] four times, work Cable Pattern in established pattern, 1hdc. Turn. – [54, 54, 54, 54, 54) sts].

For size 6 months ONLY, go to row 12.

For sizes 1 year, 2 years, 4 years, and 6 years ONLY

Row 8: Ch2, work Cable Pattern in established pattern, [2hdc in hdc, 7shdc] four times, work Cable Pattern in established pattern, 1hdc. [- (-, 58, 58, 58, 58) sts].

For size 1 year ONLY, go to row 12.

For sizes 2 years, 4 years, and 6 years ONLY

Row 9: Ch2, work Cable Pattern in established pattern, [8shdc, 2hdc in hdc] four times, work Cable Pattern in established pattern, 1hdc. Turn. [- (-, -, 62, 62, 62) sts].

For size 2 years ONLY, go to row 12.

For sizes 4 years and 6 years ONLY

Row 10: Ch2, work Cable Pattern in established pattern, [2hdc in hdc, 9shdc] four times, work Cable Pattern in established pattern, 1hdc. Turn. [- (-, -, -, 66, 66) sts].

For size 4 years ONLY, go to row 12.

For size 6 years ONLY

Row 11: Ch2, work Cable Pattern in established pattern, [10shdc, 2hdc in hdc] four times, work Cable Pattern in established pattern, 1hdc. Turn. [- (-, -, -, -, 70) sts].

For ALL sizes

Rows 12–18 (23, 24, 26, 27, 29): Ch2, work Cable Pattern in established pattern, 28 (32, 36, 40, 44, 48)shdc, work Cable Pattern in established pattern, 1hdc. Turn. [50 (54, 58, 62, 66, 70) sts].

Row 19 (24, 25, 27, 28, 30): Ch2, work Cable Pattern in established pattern, work in shdc making 5shdc2tog evenly spaced across the row, work Cable Pattern in established pattern, 1hdc. Turn. [45 (49, 53, 57, 61, 65) sts].

Row 20 (25, 26, 28, 29, 31): Ch2, work Cable Pattern in established pattern, 23 (27, 31, 35, 39, 43)shdc, work Cable Pattern in established pattern, 1hdc. Turn. [45 (49, 53, 57, 61, 65) sts].

Row 21 (26, 27, 29, 30, 32): Ch2, work Cable Pattern in established pattern, work in shdc making 5 (4, 3, 1, 4, 5) shdc2tog evenly spaced across the row, work Cable Pattern in est patt, 1hdc. Turn. [40 (45, 50, 56, 57, 60) sts].

Rows 22 (27, 28, 30, 31, 33) – 23 (29, 33, 37, 43, 43): Ch2, work Cable Pattern in established pattern, 18 (23, 28, 34, 35, 38)shdc, work Cable Pattern in established pattern, 1hdc. Turn. [40 (45, 50, 56, 57, 60) sts].

For size 6 years ONLY

Row 44: Ch2, work Cable Pattern in

established pattern, make 3shdc2tog evenly spaced across the row, work Cable Pattern in established pattern, 1hdc. Turn. [- (-, -, -, -, 57) sts].

Row 45: Ch2, work Cable Pattern in established pattern, 35hdc, work Cable Pattern in established pattern, 1hdc. Turn. [- (-, -, -, -, 57) sts].

Neck to Armhole

Row 1 (RS): Ch2, work Cable Pattern for the Front and Hood in established pattern, 0 (0, 2, 3, 3, 3)shdc, (1hdc, ch1, 1hdc) in shdc, 2 (4, 3, 4, 4, 4)shdc, (1hdc, ch1, 1hdc) in shdc, 9 (10, 13, 15, 16, 16) shdc, (1hdc, ch1, 1hdc) in shdc, 2 (4, 3, 4, 4, 4)shdc, (1hdc, ch1, 1hdc) in shdc, 1 (1, 3, 4, 4, 4)shdc, work Cable Pattern in established pattern, 1hdc. Turn. [44 (49, 54, 60, 61, 61) sts].

Rows 2–15 (17, 19, 19, 21, 23): Ch2, work Cable Pattern in established pattern, 1shdc in each shdc, (1hdc, ch, 1hdc) in each chsp for 16 (18, 20, 20, 22, 24) rows. Turn. [108 (121, 134, 140, 149, 157) sts].

Row 16 (18, 20, 20, 22, 24): (This row will separate the sleeves from the body) ch2, work Cable Pattern in established pattern, 10 (11, 14, 15, 16, 17)shdc, 6 (5, 6, 6, 7, 7)fhdc, sk 19 (23, 24, 25, 27, 29) sts, 28 (31, 36, 38, 41, 43)shdc, 6 (5, 6, 6, 7, 7) fhdc, sk 19 (23, 24, 25, 27, 29) sts, 10 (11, 14, 15, 16, 17) shdc, work Cable Pattern in established pattern, 1hdc. Turn. [82 (85, 98, 102, 109, 113) sts].

Rows 17 (19, 21, 21, 23, 25) – 44 (48, 50, 53, 57, 61): Work in established pattern.

Break yarn and weave in ends.

Sleeves (Make 2)

Turn your work at the end of each round.

Round 1: Join yarn in the middle of the fhdc on the chain side, ch2 (counts as 1hdc), 24 (27, 29, 30, 33, 35) shdc around. Join with a slst in the top of the ch2. Turn. [25 (28, 30, 31, 34, 36) sts].

Rounds 2–18 (21, 23, 26, 33, 39): Cont in est patt.

Round 19 (22, 24, 27, 34, 40): Ch2, sk 1 (-, -, 1, -, -) st, *1FPdc, 1BPdc; rep from * to end. Join. Do NOT turn. [25 (28, 30, 31, 34, 36) sts].

Round 20 (23, 25, 28, 35, 41): Ch2, *1FPdc, 1BPdc; rep from * to end. Join. Break yarn and weave in ends.

Ears (Make 4)

Ch10.

Row 1: Starting with 2nd chain from hook, 9sc. Turn [9sc].

Row 2: 1sc, 1sc2tog, 6sc. Turn. [8sc].

Row 3: 1sc, 1sc2tog, 5sc. Turn. [7sc].

Row 4: 1sc, 1sc2tog, 4sc. Turn. [6sc].

Row 5: 1sc, 1sc2tog, 3sc. Turn. [5sc].

Row 6: 1sc, 1sc2tog, 2sc. Turn. [4sc].

Row 7: 1sc, 1sc2tog, 1sc. Turn. [3sc].

Row 8: 1sc, 1sc2tog. Turn. [2sc].

Row 9: 1sc2tog. [1sc].

Break yarn and weave in ends onto one side of the ears.

Hold two triangles together, with the sides with the ends woven in facing each other and all of the corresponding edges lined up. Starting at the corner where the bottom meets the sides, sc up to the point, making a sc on the edge of each row. When you reach the top point of the triangle (sc, ch2, sc) in the top stitch, sc back down the other side of the triangle. Break off yarn, leaving an 8in tail for sewing.

Using the photo for placement, sew your wolf ears on to the top of the hood. Weave in ends.

Edging and Buttonholes

Join yarn at bottom right front corner, RS facing to work up the front of the jacket.

[Sc in the end of each row for 2in, ch4, sc in next row (one buttonhole made)] 6 (6, 7, 7, 8, 8 times).

Continue working sc around the front of the hood.

On the opposite side to the buttonholes, make one single buttonhole, approx. 3in down from the neck.

Continue working sc down the front of the jacket and around the bottom, back to where the yarn was joined. Break yarn and weave in ends.

Using the photo and buttonholes as a guide for placement, sew on buttons on the far side of opposite cable to buttonholes so that the cable overlaps fully.

THE PLAY ROOM

STAR RUG

This fresh twist on a traditional rag rug will add
a touch of fun to any nursery.

skill level:
intermediate

Size	One size
Width	51in
Yarn amounts	352yd

MATERIALS:
- Using 17½oz cones of Hooplayarn (recycled jersey cotton), 109yd/cone Main Color (MC): 52½oz Grey Marl
- Color A: 17½oz Neon Green
- Color B: 3½oz Aqua Blue
- Color C: 3½oz Darkest Blue
- M13/9.00mm Hook

YARN REVIEW:
Made from waste from the textile industry, this jersey T-shirt yarn makes a hard-wearing (and eco-friendly) rug.

YARN ALTERNATIVES:
Zapetti
Idle Hands T-shirt Yarn

GAUGE:
Work 10 sts and 2.5 rows in double crochet to measure 4in square with M13/9mm hook, or size required to obtain gauge.

SPECIAL STITCHES:
Modified Shell (ModShell)
(3dc, 1tr, 3dc) in the same stitch

Single Crochet Three Together (sc3tog)
[Insert hook in next stitch, YO and pull through stitch] three times (four loops on hook), YO and pull through all four loops.

PATTERN NOTES:
Do not turn your work at the end of each round.

INSTRUCTIONS:

Using MC, ch1 (does not count as a st), [1sc, ch1] five times into a magic loop. Join. [5sc].

Round 1: Ch1 (does not count as a st), *2sc in sc, 2sc in chsp; rep from * to end. Join in first sc. [20sc].

Round 2: Ch1 (does not count as a st, 1sc, [sk 1 st, (2dc, 1tr, 2dc) in next sc, sk 1 st, 1sc] four times, sk 1, (2dc, 1tr, 2dc) in sc, sk 1 st, slst in first sc. [30 sts].

Round 3: Ch3 (counts as 1dc), 1dc, ModShell in tr, 2dc, 1sc, * 2dc, ModShell in tr, 2dc, 1sc; rep from * to end. Join in top of ch3. Break yarn. [60 sts].

Round 4: Switch to Color A, 1slst to first dc, ch3 (counts as 1dc), 3dc, ModShell in tr, 4dc, sc3tog, *4dc, ModShell in tr, 4dc, sc3tog; rep from * to end. Join in top of ch3. Break yarn. [80 sts].

Round 5: Switch to Color B, 1slst to first dc, ch3 (counts as 1dc), 5dc, ModShell in tr, 6dc, sc3tog, *6dc, ModShell in tr, 6dc, sc3tog; rep from * to end. Join in top of ch3. Break yarn. [100 sts].

Round 6: Switch to Color C, 1slst to first dc, ch3 (counts as 1dc), 7dc, ModShell in tr, 8dc, sc3tog, *8dc, ModShell in tr, 8dc, sc3tog; rep from * to end. Join in top of ch3. Break yarn. [120 sts].

Round 7: Switch to MC, 1slst to first dc, ch3 (counts as 1dc), 9dc, ModShell in tr, 10dc, sc3tog, *10dc, ModShell in tr, 10dc, sc3tog; rep from * to end. Join in top of ch3. [140 sts)].

Round 8: 1slst to first dc, ch3 (counts as 1dc), 11dc, ModShell in tr, 12dc, sc3tog, *12dc, ModShell in tr, 12dc, sc3tog; rep from * to end. Join in top of ch3. [160 sts].

Round 9: 1slst to first dc, ch3 (counts as 1dc), 13dc, ModShell in tr, 13dc, sc3tog, *14dc, ModShell in tr, 14dc, sc3tog; rep from * to end. Join in top of ch3. Break yarn. [180 sts].

Round 10: Switch to Color A, 1slst to first dc, ch3 (counts as 1dc), 15dc, ModShell in tr, 16dc, sc3tog, *16dc, ModShell in tr, 16dc, sc3tog; rep from * to end. Join in top of ch3. Break yarn. [200 sts].

Round 11: Switch to Color B, 1slst to first dc, ch3 (counts as 1dc), 17dc, ModShell in tr, 18dc, sc3tog, *18dc, ModShell in tr, 18dc, sc3tog; rep from * to end. Join in top of ch3. Break yarn. [220 sts].

Round 12: Switch to Color C, 1slst to first dc, ch3 (counts as 1dc), 19dc, ModShell in tr, 20dc, sc3tog, *20dc, ModShell in tr, 20dc, sc3tog; rep from * to end. Join in top of ch3. Break yarn. [240 sts].

Round 13: Switch to MC, 1slst to first dc, ch3 (counts as 1dc), 21dc, ModShell in tr, 22dc, sc3tog, *22dc, ModShell in tr, 22dc, sc3tog; rep from * to end. Join in top of ch3. [260 sts].

Round 14: 1slst to first dc, ch3 (counts as 1dc), 23dc, ModShell in tr, 24dc, sc3tog, *24dc, ModShell in tr, 24dc, sc3tog; rep from * to end. Join in top of ch3. [280 sts].

Break yarn and weave in ends with your crochet hook.

SLEEPY OCTOPUS

This is the perfect companion for all the undersea adventures that may occur in dreamland, though be aware: She snores.

skill level:
intermediate

Size	One size
Width	18in
Yarn amounts	372yd

MATERIALS:

- Cygnet Seriously Chunky (100% acrylic), 52.5yd/ball
- Main Color (MC): 31½oz Burnt Orange (4888)
- Contrast Color (CC): 3½oz Black (217)
- M13/9.00mm hook
- Toy stuffing or a pillow measuring approximately 18in across (square will work if you can't find a round one)
- 16in zipper in a co-ordinating color
- Tapestry needle
- Sewing needle
- Co-ordinating thread
  Stitch marker

YARN REVIEW:

Soft and washable, this affordable yarn is a great option for room decorations.

YARN ALTERNATIVES:

Sirdar Big Softie Super Chunky
Cascade Magnum

GAUGE:

Work 9 sts and 8 rounds in single crochet to measure 4in square using M13/9mm hook, or size required to obtain gauge.

PATTERN NOTES:

This pattern is worked entirely in the round in the amigurumi style, with no seams or turning chains at the start of the rounds. Mark the beginning of your rounds with a stitch marker.

INSTRUCTIONS:

Legs (Make 8)

Using MC, leave a 6in tail, ch1
(does not count as a st) and 5sc into
a magic loop. [5sc].

Round 1: 5sc.

Round 2: 2sc in sc, 1sc, sc2tog, 1sc.
[5sc].

Rounds 3–13: (It is easiest to work this
section in a spiral, rather than keeping
track of stitch counts per round) 1sc, 2sc
in the middle of the 'V' where you made
2sc in the previous round, 1sc, sc2tog
working on either side of the sc2tog
of the previous round, 1sc. [5sc].

Round 14: [2sc in sc] twice, placing
stitch marker in first sc, 3sc. [7sc].
Move stitch marker in the first stitch
of each round.

Round 15: 2sc, [2sc in next sc] twice,
3sc. [9sc].

Round 16: 3sc, [2sc in next sc] twice,
4sc. [11sc].

Rounds 17–21: 11sc.

Round 22: 1sc, sc2tog, 6sc, sc2tog.
[9sc].

Round 23: sc2tog, 3sc, 2sc in next sc,
3sc. [9sc].

Round 24: sc2tog, 7sc. [8sc].

Rounds 25–28: 8sc.

Thread the beginning tail onto a tapestry
needle. Weave the yarn up through
the stitches on the side of the leg that
naturally curls in, pulling gently as you
go to accentuate the curve of the leg.
Once you reach the increase section,
bring yarn to inside of the leg and tie
off neatly inside the leg.

Cushion (Makes 2)

Using MC, ch1 (does not count as
a stitch), 6sc into a magic loop. [6sc].

Round 1: *2sc in sc; rep from * around.
[12sc].

Round 2: *2sc in sc, 1sc; rep from *
around. [18sc].

Round 3: *2sc in sc, 2sc; rep from *
around. [24sc].

Round 4: *2sc in sc, 3sc; rep from *
around. [30sc].

Round 5: *2sc in sc, 4sc; rep from *
around. [36sc].

Round 6: *2sc in sc, 5sc; rep from *
around. [42sc].

Round 7: *2sc in sc, 6sc; rep from *
around. [48sc].

Round 8: *2sc in sc, 7sc; rep from *
around. [54sc].

Round 8: *2sc in sc, 8sc; rep from *
around. [60sc].

Round 9: *2sc in sc, 9sc; rep from *
around. [66sc].

Round 10: *2sc in sc, 10sc; rep from *
around. [72sc].

Round 11: *2sc in sc, 11sc; rep from *
around. [78sc].

Round 12: *2sc in sc, 12sc; rep from *
around. [84sc].

Round 13: *2sc in sc, 13sc; rep from *
around. [90sc].

Round 14: *2sc in sc, 14sc; rep from *
around. [96sc].

Round 15: *2sc in sc, 15sc; rep from *
around. [102sc].

Round 16: *2sc in sc, 16sc; rep from *
around. [108sc].

Joining

You will slst around the edges. Place
the top and bottom pieces, wrong sides
together, stitches aligned. Top side facing,
make 2slst working through both layers
(all four loops) to join the sides together.

Joining with Legs

Fold the open end of tentacle in half,
stitches aligned, place it between the two
layers of the cushion.

Insert hook through top layer, then insert
hook through both layers of the tentacle,
then through the bottom side of the
cushion.

YO and pull through all layers of stitches
until you are at the top and then through
the loop on the hook.

Repeat steps 2–3 for the 3 remaining
stitches of the leg, then make 3slst,
working through both layers of the
cushion.

Repeat steps 1–4 for the three remaining
legs on that side.

Make 15 slst working through both
layers of the cushion.

Repeat steps 1–4 for three legs on the
other side of the pillow.

Repeat steps 1–4 for the final leg, but
make only 2slst after the final leg. Break
yarn and weave in ends.

Insert zipper into opening of the pillow.
Using a sewing needle, hand sew one
side of the zipper to the upper side of
the pillow and one side to the lower
side of the pillow, opening the zipper as
needed. Stuff cushion with toy stuffing
or pillow.

Note: If you don't want to add a zipper,
simply slst the pillow closed. [108slst].

Eyes

Using the photo as a guide, thread a
tapestry needle with CC. Embroider the
eyes using a back stitch (see Techniques
and Basic Stitches on page 15) for the
eyelid and then five short stitches for
the eyelashes.

BUNTING BABY BLANKET

The bright colors of strung bunting will liven up any nursery.

MATERIALS:

- ◉ 1¾oz balls of Milla Mia DK (100% superwash merino wool), 137yd/ball Main Color (MC): 21oz Snow (124)
- ◉ Color B: 3½oz Storm (102)
- ◉ Color C: 1¾oz Scarlet (140)
- ◉ Color D: 1¾oz Daisy (142)
- ◉ Color E: 1¾oz Grass (141)
- ◉ Color F: 1¾oz Peacock (144)
- ◉ Color G: 1¾oz Fuchsia (143)
- ◉ G6/4.00mm hook
- ◉ Tapestry needle

YARN ALTERNATIVES:
Rowan Pure Wool DK
Patons Fab DK

GAUGE:
Work 18sts and 18 rows in sc to measure 4in square using G6/4mm hook, or size required to obtain gauge.

PATTERN NOTES:

• This pattern is a colorwork/tapestry crochet pattern. To ensure the neatest finish possible, you will carry MC across the colored bunting triangles by holding it on top of the stitches in the previous row and crocheting around it with your working yarn. This is also a useful method to deal with your wool ends without having to weave them in later.

• You will drop each other color when you switch to the MC in between each flag. You will leave it hanging and pick it up when you come to it on the next row.

• You will always switch colors when you have two loops from your previous sc on your hook (see Techniques and Basic Stitches on page 14). Do not count the ch1 at the beginning of the row as a stitch.

INSTRUCTIONS:

Using MC, ch157.

Row 1: Starting with the 2nd chain from hook, 156sc. Turn. [156sc].

Rows 2–4: Ch1. sc across. Turn. [156sc].

Rows 5–6: Switch to Color B. ch1. sc across. Turn.

Row 7: (You will need two separate balls of Color F in this row for two half flags.) Join Color F. ch1, 12sc. Switch to MC, 1sc. Switch to Color E, 25sc. Switch to MC, 1sc. Switch to Color D, 25sc. Switch to MC, 1sc. Switch to Color C, 25sc. Switch to MC, 1sc. Switch to Color B, 25sc. Switch to MC, 1sc. Switch to Color G, 25sc. Switch to MC, 1sc. Switch to Color F, 13sc. Turn.

Row 8: In Color F, ch1, 12sc. Switch to MC, 3sc. Switch to Color G, 23sc. Switch to MC, 3sc. Switch to Color B, 23sc. Switch to MC, 3sc. Switch to Color C, 23sc. Switch to MC, 3sc. Switch to Color D, 23sc. Switch to MC, 3sc. Switch to Color E, 23sc. Switch to MC, 3sc. Switch to Color F, 11sc. Turn.

Row 9: In Color F, ch1, 11sc. Switch to MC, 3sc. Switch to Color E, 23sc. Switch to MC, 3sc. Switch to Color D, 23sc. Switch to MC, 3sc. Switch to Color C, 23sc. Switch to MC, 3sc. Switch to Color B, 23sc. Switch to MC, 3sc. Switch to Color G, 23sc. Switch to MC, 3sc. Switch to Color F, 12sc. Turn.

Row 10: In Color F, ch1, 11sc. Switch to MC, 5sc. Switch to Color G, 21sc. Switch to MC, 5sc. Switch to Color B, 21sc. Switch to MC, 5sc. Switch to Color C, 21sc. Switch to MC, 5sc. Switch to Color D, 21sc. Switch to MC, 5sc. Switch to Color E, 21sc. Switch to MC, 5sc. Switch to Color F, 10sc. Turn.

Row 11: In Color F, ch1, 10sc. Switch to MC, 5sc. Switch to Color E, 21sc. Switch to MC, 5sc. Switch to Color D, 21sc. Switch to MC, 5sc. Switch to Color C, 21sc. Switch to MC, 5sc. Switch to Color B, 21sc. Switch to MC, 5sc. Switch to Color G, 21sc. Switch to MC, 5sc. Switch to Color F, 11sc. Turn.

Row 12: In Color F, ch1, 10sc. Switch to MC, 7sc. Switch to Color G, 19sc. Switch to MC, 7sc. Switch to Color B, 19sc. Switch to MC, 7sc. Switch to Color C, 19sc. Switch to MC, 7sc. Switch to Color D, 19sc. Switch to MC, 7sc. Switch to Color E, 19sc. Switch to MC, 7sc. Switch to Color F, 9sc. Turn.

Row 13: In Color F, ch1, 9sc. Switch to MC, 7sc. Switch to Color E, 19sc. Switch to MC, 7sc. Switch to Color D, 19sc. Switch to MC, 7sc. Switch to Color C, 19sc. Switch to MC, 7sc. Switch to Color B, 19sc. Switch to MC, 7sc. Switch to Color G, 19sc. Switch to MC, 7sc. Switch to Color F, 10sc. Turn.

Row 14: In Color F, ch1, 9sc. Switch to MC, 9sc. Switch to Color G, 17sc. Switch to MC, 9sc. Switch to Color B, 17sc. Switch to MC, 9sc. Switch to Color C, 17sc. Switch to MC, 9sc.

Switch to Color D, 17sc. Switch to MC, 9sc. Color E, 17sc. Switch to MC, 9sc. Switch to Color F, 8sc. Turn.

Row 15: In Color F, ch1, 8sc. Switch to MC, 9sc. Switch to Color E, 17sc. Switch to MC, 9sc. Switch to Color D, 17sc. Switch to MC, 9sc. Switch to Color C, 17sc. Switch to MC, 9sc. Switch to Color B, 17sc. Switch to MC, 9sc. Switch to Color G, 17sc. Switch to MC, 9sc. Switch to Color F, 9sc. Turn.

Row 16: In Color F, ch1, 8sc. Switch to MC, 11sc. Switch to Color G, 15sc. Switch to MC, 11sc. Switch to Color B, 15sc. Switch to MC, 11sc. Switch to Color C, 15sc. Switch to MC, 11sc. Switch to Color D, 15sc. Switch to MC, 11sc. Switch to Color E, 15sc. Switch to MC, 11sc. Switch to Color F, 7sc. Turn.

Row 17: In Color F, ch1, 7sc. Switch to MC, 11sc. Switch to Color E, 15sc. Switch to MC, 11sc. Switch to Color D, 15sc. Switch to MC, 11sc. Switch to Color C, 15sc. Switch to MC, 11sc. Switch to Color B, 15sc. Switch to MC, 11sc. Switch to Color G, 15sc. Switch to MC, 11sc. Switch to Color F 8sc. Turn.

Row 18: In Color F, ch1, 8sc. Switch to MC, 11sc. Switch to Color G, 15sc. Switch to MC, 11sc. Switch to Color B, 15sc. Switch to MC, 11sc. Switch to Color C, 15sc. Switch to MC, 11sc. Switch to Color D, 15sc. Switch to MC, 11sc. Switch to Color E, 15sc. Switch to MC, 11sc. Switch to Color F, 7sc. Turn.

Row 19: In Color F, ch1, 6sc. Switch to MC, 13sc. Switch to Color E, 13sc Switch to MC, 13sc. Switch to Color D, 13sc. Switch to MC, 13sc. Switch to Color C, 13sc. Switch to MC, 13sc. Switch to Color B, 13sc. Switch to MC, 13sc. Switch to Color G, 13sc. Switch to MC, 13sc. Switch to Color F, 7sc. Turn.

Row 20: In Color F, ch1, 7sc. Switch to MC, 13sc. Switch to Color G, 13sc. Switch to MC, 13sc. Switch to Color B, 13sc. Switch to MC, 13sc. Switch to Switch to Color C, 13sc. Switch to MC, 13sc. Switch to Color D, 13sc. Switch to MC, 13sc. Switch to Color E, 13sc. Switch to MC, 13sc. Switch to Color F, 6sc. Turn.

Row 21: In Color F, ch1, 5sc. Switch to MC, 15sc. Switch to Color E, 11sc. Switch to MC, 15sc. Switch to Color D, 11sc. Switch to MC, 15sc. Switch to Color C, 11sc. Switch to MC, 15sc. Switch to Color B, 11sc. Switch to MC, 15sc. Switch to Color G, 11sc. Switch to MC, 15sc. Switch to Color F, 6sc. Turn.

Row 22: In Color F, ch1, 6sc. Switch to

MC, 15sc. Switch to Color G, 11sc. Switch to MC, 15sc. Switch to Color B, 11sc. Switch to MC, 15sc. Switch to Color C, 11sc. Switch to MC, 15sc. Switch to Color D, 11sc. Switch to MC, 15sc. Switch to Color E, 11sc. Switch to MC, 15sc. Switch to Color F, 5sc. Turn.

Row 23: In Color F, ch1, 4sc. Switch to MC, 17sc. Switch to Color E, 9sc. Switch to MC, 17sc. Switch to Color D, 9sc. Switch to MC, 17sc. Switch to Color C, 9sc. Switch to MC, 17sc. Switch to Color B, 9sc. Switch to MC, 17sc. Switch to Color G, 9sc. Switch to MC, 15sc. Switch to Color F, 5sc. Turn.

Row 24: In Color F, ch1, 5sc. Switch to MC, 17sc. Switch to Color G, 9sc. Switch to MC, 17sc. Switch to Color B, 9sc. Switch to MC, 17sc. Switch to Color C, 9sc. Switch to MC, 17sc. Switch to Color D, 9sc. Switch to MC, 17sc. Switch to Color E, 9sc. Switch to MC, 17sc. Switch to Color F, 4sc. Turn.

Row 25: In Color F, ch1, 3sc. Switch to MC, 19sc. Switch to Color E, 7sc. Switch to MC, 19sc. Switch to Color D, 7sc. Switch to MC, 19sc. Switch to Color C, 7sc. Switch to MC, 19sc. Switch to Color B, 7sc. Switch to MC, 19sc. Switch to Color G, 7sc. Switch to MC, 19sc. Switch to Color F, 4sc. Turn.

Row 26: In Color F, ch1, 4sc. Switch to MC, 19sc. Switch to Color G, 7sc. Switch to MC, 19sc. Switch to Color B, 7sc. Switch to MC, 19sc. Switch to Color C, 7sc. Switch to MC, 19sc.

Switch to Color D, 7sc. Switch to MC, 19sc. Switch to Color E, 7sc. Switch to MC, 19sc. Switch to Color F, 3sc. Turn.

Row 27: In Color F, ch1, 2sc. Switch to MC, 21sc. Switch to Color E, 5sc. Switch to MC, 21sc. Switch to Color D, 5sc. Switch to MC, 21sc. Switch to Color C, 5sc. Switch to MC, 21sc. Switch to Color B, 5sc. Switch to MC, 21sc. Switch to Color G, 5sc. Switch to MC, 21sc. Switch to Color F, 3sc. Turn.

Row 28: In Color F, ch1, 3sc. Switch to MC, 21sc. Switch to Color G, 5sc. Switch to MC, 21sc. Switch to Color B, 5sc. Switch to MC, 21sc. Switch to Color C, 5sc. Switch to MC, 21sc. Switch to Color D, 5sc. Switch to MC, 21sc. Switch to Color E, 5sc. Switch to MC, 21sc. Switch to Color F, 2sc. Turn.

Row 29: In Color F, ch1, 1sc. Switch to MC, 23sc. Switch to Color E, 3sc. Switch to MC, 23sc. Switch to Color D, 3sc. Switch to MC, 23sc. Switch to Color C, 3sc. Switch to MC, 23sc. Switch to Color B, 3sc. Switch to MC, 23sc. Switch to Color G, 3sc. Switch to MC, 23sc. Switch to Color F, 2sc. Turn.

Row 30: In Color F, ch1, 2sc. Switch to MC, 23sc. Switch to Color G, 3sc. Switch to MC, 23sc. Switch to Color B, 3sc. Switch to MC, 23sc. Switch to Color C, 3sc. Switch to MC, 23sc. Switch to Color D, 3sc. Switch to M 23sc. Switch to Color E, 3sc. Switch to MC, 23sc. Switch to Color F, 1sc. Turn.

Row 31: (On this row, break colors as you go.) Switch to MC, ch1, 25sc.

Switch to Color E, 1sc. Switch to MC 25sc. Switch to Color D, 1sc. Switch to MC, 25sc. Switch to Color C, 1sc. Switch to MC, 25sc. Switch to Color B, 1sc. Switch to MC, 25sc. Switch to Color G, 1sc. Switch to MC, 25sc. Switch to Color F, 1sc. Turn.

Rows 32–45: Switch to MC. ch1. sc across. Turn.

Row 46: In MC, ch1, 13sc. Switch to Color C, 1sc. Switch to MC, 25sc. Switch to Color D, 1sc. Switch to MC, 25sc. Switch to Color E, 1sc. Switch to MC, 25sc. Switch to Color F, 1sc. Switch to MC, 25sc. Switch to Color G, 1sc. Switch to MC, 25sc. Switch to Color B, 1sc. Switch to MC, 12sc. Turn.

Row 47: In MC, ch1, 11sc. Switch to Color B, 3sc. Switch to MC, 23sc. Switch to Color G, 3sc. Switch to MC, 23sc. Switch to Color F, 3sc. Switch to MC, 23sc. Switch to Color E, 3sc. Switch to MC, 23sc. Switch to Color D, 3sc. Switch to MC, 23sc. Switch to Color C, 3sc. Switch to MC, 12sc. Turn.

Row 48: In MC, ch1, 12sc. Switch to Color C, 3sc. Switch to MC, 23sc. Switch to Color D, 3sc. Switch to MC, 23sc. Switch to Color E, 3sc. Switch to MC, 23sc. Switch to Color F, 3sc. Switch to MC, 23sc. Switch to Color G, 3sc. Switch to MC, 23sc Switch to Color B, 3sc. Switch to MC, 11sc. Turn.

Row 49: In MC, ch1, 10sc. Switch to Color B, 5sc. Switch to MC, 21sc. Switch to Color G, 5sc. Switch to MC,

21sc. Switch to Color F, 5sc. Switch to MC, 21sc. Switch to Color E, 5sc. Switch to MC, 21sc. Switch to Color D, 5sc. Switch to MC, 21sc. Switch to Color C, 5sc. Switch to MC, 11sc.

Row 50: In MC, ch1, 11sc. Switch to Color C, 5sc. Switch to MC, 21sc. Switch to Color D, 5sc. Switch to MC, 21sc. Switch to Color E, 5sc. Switch to MC, 21sc. Switch to Color F, 5sc. Switch to MC, 21sc. Switch to Color G, 5sc. Switch to MC, 21sc. Switch to Color B, 5sc. Switch to MC, 10sc. Turn.

Row 51: In MC, ch1, 9sc. Switch to Color B, 7sc. Switch to MC, 19sc. Switch to Color G, 7sc. Switch to MC, 19sc. Switch to Color F, 7sc. Switch to MC, 19sc. Switch to Color E, 7sc. Switch to MC, 19sc. Switch to Color D, 7sc. Switch to MC, 19sc. Switch to Color C, 7sc. Switch to MC, 10sc. Turn.

Row 52: In MC, ch1, 10sc. Switch to Color C, 7sc. Switch to MC, 19sc. Switch to Color D, 7sc. Switch to MC, 19sc. Switch to Color E, 7sc. Switch to MC, 19sc. Switch to Color F, 7sc. Switch to MC, 19sc. Switch to Color G, 7sc. Switch to MC, 19sc. Switch to Color B, 7sc. Switch to MC, 9sc. Turn.

Row 53: In MC, ch1, 8sc. Switch to Color B, 9sc. Switch to MC, 17sc. Switch to Color G, 9sc. Switch to MC, 17sc. Switch to Color F, 9sc. Switch to MC, 17sc. Switch to Color E, 9sc. Switch to MC, 17sc. Switch to Color D, 9sc. Switch to MC, 17sc. Switch to Color C, 9sc. Switch to MC, 9sc. Turn.

Row 54: In MC, ch1, 9sc. Switch to

Color C, 9sc. Switch to MC, 17sc. Switch to Color D, 9sc. Switch to MC, 17sc. Switch to Color E, 9sc. Switch to MC, 17sc. Switch to Color F, 9sc. Switch to MC, 17sc. Switch to Color G, 9sc. Switch to MC, 17sc. Switch to Color B. 9sc. Switch to MC, 8sc. Turn.

Row 55: In MC, ch1, 7sc. Switch to Color B, 11sc. Switch to MC, 15sc. Switch to Color G, 11sc. Switch to MC, 15sc. Switch to Color F, 11sc. Switch to MC, 15sc. Switch to Color E, 11sc. Switch to MC, 15sc. Switch to Color D, 11sc. Switch to MC, 15sc. Switch to Color C, 11sc. Switch to MC, 8sc. Turn.

Row 56: In MC, ch1, 8sc. Switch to Color C, 11sc. Switch to MC, 15sc. Switch to Color D, 11sc. Switch to MC, 15sc. Switch to Color E, 11sc. Switch to MC, 15sc. Switch to Color F, 11sc. Switch to MC, 15sc. Switch to Color G, 11sc. Switch to MC, 15sc Switch to Color B, 11sc. Switch to MC, 7sc. Turn.

Row 57: In MC, ch1, 6sc. Switch to Color B, 13sc. Switch to MC, 13sc. Switch to Color G, 13sc. Switch to MC, 13sc. Switch to Color F, 13sc. Switch to MC, 13sc. Switch to Color E, 13sc. Switch to MC, 13sc. Switch to Color D, 13sc. Switch to MC, 13sc. Switch to Color C, 13sc. Switch to MC, 7sc. Turn.

Row 58: In MC, ch1, 7sc. Switch to Color C, 13sc. Switch to MC, 13sc. Switch to Color D, 13sc. Switch to MC, 13sc. Switch to Color E, 13sc. Switch to MC, 13sc. Switch to Color

F, 13sc. Switch to MC, 13sc. Switch to Color G, 13sc. Switch to MC, 13sc Switch to Color B, 13sc. Switch to MC, 6sc.

Row 59: In MC, ch1, 5sc. Switch to Color B, 15sc. Switch to MC, 11sc. Switch to Color G, 15sc. Switch to MC, 11sc. Switch to Color F, 15sc. Switch to MC, 11sc. Switch to Color E. 15sc. Switch to MC, 11sc. Switch to Color D, 15sc. Switch to MC, 11sc. Switch to Color C, 15sc. Switch to MC, 6sc. Turn.

Row 60: In MC, ch1, 6sc. Switch to Color C, 15sc. Switch to MC, 11sc. Switch to Color D, 15sc. Switch to MC, 11sc. Switch. Switch to MC, 11sc. Switch to Color F, 15sc. Switch to MC, 11sc. Switch to Color G, 15sc. Switch to MC, 11sc. Switch to Color B, 15sc.

Switch to MC, 5sc. Turn.

Row 61: In MC, ch1, 5sc. Switch to Color B, 15sc. Switch to MC, 11sc. Switch to Color G, 15sc. Switch to MC, 11sc. Switch to Color F, 15sc. Switch to MC, 11sc. Switch to Color E, 15sc. Switch to MC, 11sc. Switch to Color D, 15sc. Switch to MC, 11sc. Switch to Color C, 15sc. Switch to MC, 6sc. Turn.

Row 62: In MC, ch1, 5sc. Switch to Color C, 17sc. Switch to MC, 9sc. Switch to Color D, 17sc. Switch to MC, 9sc. Switch to Color E, 17sc. Switch to MC, 9sc. Switch to Color F, 17sc. Switch to MC, 9sc. Switch to Color G, 17sc. Switch to MC, 9sc. Switch to Color B, 17sc. Switch to MC, 4sc. Turn.

Row 63: In MC, ch1, 4sc. Switch to Color B, 17sc. Switch to MC, 9sc. Switch to Color G, 17sc. Switch to MC, 9sc. Switch to Color F, 17sc. Switch to MC, 9sc. Switch to Color E, 17sc. Switch to MC, 9sc. Switch to Color D, 17sc. Switch to MC, 9sc. Switch to Color C, 17sc. Switch to MC, 5sc. Turn.

Row 64: In MC, ch1, 4sc. Switch to Color C, 19sc. Switch to MC, 7sc. Switch to Color D, 19sc. Switch to MC, 7sc. Switch to Color E, 19sc. Switch to MC, 7sc. Switch to Color F, 19sc. Switch to MC, 7sc. Switch to Color G, 19sc. Switch to MC, 7sc. Switch to Color B, 19sc. Switch to MC, 3sc.

Row 65: In MC, ch1, 3sc. Switch to Color B, 19sc. Switch to MC, 7sc.

Switch to Color G, 19sc. Switch to MC, 7sc. Switch to Color F, 19sc. Switch to MC, 7sc. Switch to Color E, 19sc. Switch to MC, 7sc. Switch to Color D, 19sc. Switch to MC, 7sc. Switch to Color C, 19sc. Switch to MC, 4sc. Turn.

Row 66: In MC, ch1, 3sc. Switch to Color C, 21sc. Switch to MC, 5sc. Switch to Color D, 21sc. Switch to MC, 5sc. Switch to Color E, 21sc. Switch to MC, 5sc. Switch to Color F, 21sc. Switch to MC, 5sc. Switch to Color G, 21sc. Switch to MC, 5sc. Switch to Color B, 21sc. Switch to MC, 2sc. Turn.

Row 67: In MC, ch1, 2sc. Switch to Color B, 21sc. Switch to MC, 5sc. Switch to Color G, 21sc. Switch to MC, 5sc. Switch to Color F, 21sc. Switch to MC, 5sc. Switch to Color E, 21sc. Switch to MC, 5sc. Switch to Color D, 21sc. Switch to MC, 5sc. Switch to Color C, 21sc. Switch to MC, 3sc. Turn.

Row 68: In MC, ch1, 2sc. Switch to Color C, 23sc. Switch to MC, 3sc. Switch to Color D, 23sc. Switch to MC, 3sc. Switch to Color E, 23sc. Switch to MC, 3sc. Switch to Color F, 23sc. Switch to MC, 3sc. Switch to Color G, 23sc. Switch to MC, 3sc. Switch to Color B, 23sc. Switch to MC, 1sc. Turn.

Row 69: In MC, ch1, sc. Switch to Color B, 23sc. Switch to MC, 3sc. Switch to Color G, 23sc. Switch to MC, 3sc. Switch to Color F, 23sc. Switch to MC, 3sc. Switch to Color

E, 23sc. Switch to MC, 3sc. Switch to Color D, 23sc. Switch to MC, 3sc. Switch to Color C, 23sc. Switch to MC, 2sc. Turn.

Row 70: (On this row, break colors as you go.) In MC, ch1, 1sc. Switch to Color C, 25sc. Switch to MC, 1sc. Switch to Color D, 25sc. Switch to MC, 1sc. Switch to Color E, 25sc. Switch to MC, 1sc. Switch to Color F, 25sc. Switch to MC, 1sc. Switch to Color G, 25sc. Switch to MC, 1sc.

Switch to Color B, 25sc. Turn.

Rows 71–72: Continuing in Color B. ch1, sc across. Break Color B. Turn.

Rows 73–76: Switch to MC. ch1, sc across. Turn.

Repeat rows 1–76 twice more.

Bind off and weave in any additional ends.

BLACK-EYED SUSAN BABY BLANKET

The Black-eyed Susan has always been my favorite flower. Bright and sunny, they grow in abundance on the roadsides of my native Iowa. This baby blanket is a very quick and very simple make, easily crocheted in front of a film for a last-minute gift, bringing these happy daisies into any nursery.

skill level: beginner

Size	One size
Finished diameter	33in
Yarn amounts	266yd

MATERIALS:

- Cascade Yarns Magnum (100% wool) 123yd/hank
- Main Color (MC): 17½oz Gold (9463B)
- Contrast Color (CC): 8¾oz Black (0050)
- P/12mm hook
- Tapestry needle

YARN REVIEW:

A lovely single-ply wool in a very thick super-bulky weight means this project flies off the hook.

YARN ALTERNATIVES:

Seriously Chunky by Cygnet

GAUGE:

Work 7¼sts and 3¼ rounds in double crochet to measure 4in square using a P/12mm hook, or size required to obtain gauge.

SPECIAL STITCHES:

Double Crochet 3 Together (dc3tog)
YO, insert hook in first stitch to decrease, YO, pull through stitch (three loops on hook). YO, insert hook through the next stitch to decrease, YO and pull through stitch (five loops on hook). YO, insert hook through the 3rd stitch to decrease, YO and pull through stitch (seven loops on hook). YO and pull through six loops. YO, pull through two remaining loops. 2sts decreased.

Pattern notes:

Constructed from the center out in a circle, the spaces created by the chain stitches show off the petals of the flower.

Do not turn your work at the end of each round.

INSTRUCTIONS:

Using CC, ch1 (does not count as a st), 6sc into a magic loop. Join. [6sc].

Round 1: Ch1, 2sc in each st around. Join. [12sc].

Round 2: Ch1, ★2sc in the same st, 1sc; rep from ★ to end. Join. [18sc].

Round 3: Ch1, ★2sc in the same st, 2sc; rep from ★ around. Join. [24sc].

Round 4: Ch4 (counts as 1sc and ch3), sk 1 st, ★1sc, ch3, sk 1 st; rep from ★ around. Join. Break yarn. [12sc].

From here forward each ch3 at the beginning of the round counts as a 1dc.

Round 5: (This round is worked into the ch3sps), join MC in first ch3sp, ch3, 3dc, ch1, ★4dc in next ch3sp, ch1; rep from ★ around. Join in the top of ch3 at the beginning of the round. [48dc].

Round 6: Ch3, [2dc in next dc] twice, 1dc, ch1, sk ch1sp, ★1dc [2dc in next dc] twice, 1dc, ch1, sk 1ch; rep from ★ around. Join. [72dc].

Round 7: Ch3, 1dc, 2dc in next dc, 3dc, ch1, sk ch1sp, ★2dc, 2dc in next dc, 3dc, ch1, sk ch1sp; rep from ★ around. Join. [84dc].

Round 8: Ch3, 2dc, 2dc in next dc, 3dc, ch1, sk ch1sp, ★3dc, 2dc in next dc, 3dc, ch1, sk ch1sp; rep from ★ around. Join. [96dc].

Round 9: Ch3, 3dc, 2dc in next dc, 3dc, ch1, sk ch1sp, ★4dc, 2dc in next dc, 3dc, ch1, sk ch1sp; rep from ★ around. Join. [108dc].

Round 10: Ch3, sk 1dc, 5dc, dc2tog, ch3, sk ch1sp, ★dc2tog, 5dc, dc2tog, ch3, sk ch1sp; rep from ★ around. Join. [84dc].

Round 11: 3ch, miss 1tr, 3tr, tr2tog, 1ch, 3tr into 3chsp, 1ch, ★tr2tog, 3tr, tr2tog, 1ch, 3tr into 3chsp, ch; repeat from ★ to end. Join. (96)tr.

Round 12: Ch3, sk 1dc, 1dc, dc2tog, ch1, sk ch1sp, 2dc in next dc, 1dc, 2dc in next dc, ch1, sk ch1sp, ★dc2tog, 1dc, dc2tog, ch1, sk ch1sp, 2dc in next dc, 1dc, 2dc in next dc, ch1, sk ch1sp; rep from ★ around. Join. [96dc].

Round 13: Ch3, dc2tog, ch1, sk ch1sp, 2dc in next dc, ch2, sk 1dc, 2dc in next dc, ch2, sk 1dc, 2dc in next dc, ch1, sk 1dc, ★dc3tog, ch1, sk ch1sp, 2dc in next dc, ch2, sk 1dc, 2dc in next dc, ch2, sk 1dc, 2dc in next dc, ch1, sk ch1sp; rep from ★ to end. Join. [84dc].

Break yarn and weave in ends. The pattern made by the chain spaces Will be most visible if the piece is lightly blocked.

HOBBY HORSE

Who doesn't love whizzing around the house on a pretend horse?
Hours of fun will be had on this lovely heirloom toy.

skill level: intermediate

Size	One size
Finished measurements (stuffed)	8 x 10in
Yarn amounts: Grey Mare	216yd
Yarn amounts: Mane	78yd
Yarn amounts: Unicorn	233yd

MATERIALS:
1¾oz balls of Wendy Mode DK (50% wool, 50% acrylic), 155yd/ball

For Grey Mare
- Main Color (MC): 3½ozFog (232)
- Color A: 1¾oz Shale (219)
- Color B: 1¾oz Coffee Bean (218)

For Unicorn
- Main Color (MC): 5¼oz Whisper White (232)

- G6/4.00mm hook
- F5.3.75mm hook
- Tapestry needle
- Toy stuffing
- 2 x buttons (1in diameter) for eyes
- Wooden dowel (½in diameter x 36in long)
- Linseed or other wood finishing oil
- Small handsaw
- Hot glue (optional)

YARN REVIEW:
Highly durable, but still lovely to work with, this sport weight 50% wool-acrylic mix is perfect for a well-loved toy that is going to be played with day in day out.

YARN ALTERNATIVES:
Patons Fab DK

GAUGE:
Work 16 sts and 13½rows in dc to measure 4in square using G6/4mm hook, or size required to obtain gauge.

INSTRUCTIONS:

Muzzle

Do not turn your work at the end of each round.

Using the larger hook and the yarn for the nose (Main Color for Unicorn, Color A for Grey Mare), ch1, 8sc into a magic loop. Join. [8sc].

Round 1: Ch1, ★2sc in sc; rep from ★ around. Join. [16sc].

Round 2: Ch1, ★2sc in next sc, 1sc; rep from ★ around. Join. [24sc].

Round 3: Ch1, ★2sc in next sc, 2sc; rep from ★ around. Join. [32sc].

Round 4: Ch1, ★2sc in next sc, 3sc; rep from ★ around. Join. [40sc].

Round 5: Ch1, ★2sc in next sc, 4sc; rep from ★ around. Join. [48sc].

Round 6: Ch1, ★2sc in next sc, 5sc; rep from ★ around. Join. [56sc].

For the Grey Mare, if you are alternating colors between the nose and the main horse, switch to MC.

This section is worked entirely in the round in the amigurumi style, with no seams or turning chains at the start of the rounds.

Rounds 7–33: 56sc. Join. Do not turn. [56sc].

Top of Head

This section is worked in rows. Turn your work at the end of each row.

Rows 1–14: Ch1, 28sc. Turn. [28sc].

Fold the last row in half, right sides together lining up the stitches, working through all four loops, 14slst to close the seam. Break yarn.

Pattern notes:
For the unicorn, there are no color changes.
The ch1 beginning the rounds and rows in this pattern does not count as a st.

Neck

This section is worked entirely in the round in the amigurumi style, with no seams or turning chains at the start of the rounds. Do not turn your work at the end of the round.

Set-up

Rejoin yarn next to where you started working in rows. Work 1sc in the end of each row around the unworked stitches from the muzzle. [56sc].

Round 1: ★sc2tog, 5sc; rep from ★ around. [48sc].

Rounds 2–25: 48sc. [48sc].

Rounds 26–33: Switch to smaller hook. ch2 (does not count as a st) ★FPdc, BPdc; rep from ★ around. [48 sts]. Break yarn.

Ears (Make 4)

With larger hook and MC for Unicorn/ Grey Mare, ch9.

Row 1: Starting with the second chain from hook, 8sc. Turn. [8sc].

Row 2: Ch1, 2sc, sc2tog, 4sc. Turn. [7sc].

Row 3: Ch1, 2sc, sc2tog, 3sc. Turn. [6sc].

Row 4: Ch1, 2sc, sc2tog, 2sc. Turn. [5sc].

Row 5: Ch1, 2sc, sc2tog, 1sc. Turn. [4sc].

Row 6: Ch1, 2sc, sc2tog. Turn. [3sc].

Row 7: Ch1, 1sc, sc2tog. Turn. [2sc].

Row 8: Sc2tog. Break yarn. [1sc].

Hold two ears together, wrong sides facing. Rejoin yarn at the edge of the beginning ch. Working in the ends of the rows, 7sc, [1sc, ch2, 1sc] in sc2tog from Row 8, 7sc down the other end of the rows. Break yarn, leaving an 8in tail for sewing on.

Unicorn Horn

This section is worked entirely in the round in the amigurumi style, with no seams or turning chains at the start of the rounds. Do not turn your work at the end of the round.

With the larger hook and the yarn for the horn, ch1 (does not count as a st), 4sc into a magic loop. [4sc].

Round 1: 4sc.

Round 2: *1sc, 2sc in next sc; rep from * around. [6sc].

Round 3: 6sc.

Round 4: *1sc, 2sc in next sc; rep from * around. [9sc].

Round 5: 9sc.

Round 6: *2sc, 2sc in next sc; rep from * around. [12sc].

Rounds 7–11: 12sc.

Break yarn, leaving a 12in tail for sewing on. Lightly stuff.

Stuffing

Stuff the full length of the head part of your horse with toy stuffing. To help minimize lumps in the horse, try and fill the head with a single piece of stuffing, rather than filling it with small pieces at a time.

Tying Mane

Using Color A for Grey Mare and MC for Unicorn, cut strips of yarn, roughly 7in in length. Fold the strips in half and, using your crochet hook, pull the loops through the space between the stitches where you want the mane. Thread the ends of the mane strips through the loop and pull tight. Repeat until the mane is as full as you want it to be.

Bridle

Using the larger crochet hook and Color B for Grey Mare and MC for Unicorn, join yarn at the underside of the muzzle of the horse on the outside of row 17 of the muzzle. Using the space between the stitches as a guide, slst on the outside of the nose around in a full circle.

Using a second length of the same yarn (either a separate length cut from the ball or pulled from the center of the skein), hold the wool double and make a chain 20in long.

Bring the long end of the reins around the back and slst to join the reins to the bridle. Weave in ends.

Sewing Up

Using the photo for placement, sew on ears and buttons for eyes. For eyelashes, cut a number of strands of wool and tie around the button. Trim to desired length.

Stick

Follow the instructions on the wood treatment oil to treat your dowel.

Using your handsaw, mark three lines 7½, 7¾ and 8¼in down from the top of the dowel. Saw three notches in the wood, approximately ¼in wide and deep all the way around the dowel at these marks.

Wrap dowel with stuffing to the point of the first notch, and add extra stuffing at the top of the horse's head. Insert dowel in neck of horse. Wrap extra yarn tightly and securely around the outside of the horse's neck repeatedly at the point of the notches to secure it to the horse. (For extra security, you can add a bit of hot glue to the dowel notches before wrapping.)

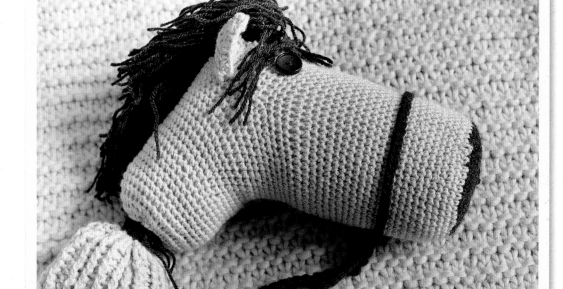

SOURCES FOR SUPPLIES

To find a local source for the yarns used in this book, contact the manufacturers below.

Adriafil Srl
Italian yarn company, offering yarns in a huge range of weights, colors and fibers.
www.adriafil.com/uk

Artesano Ltd.
Makers of Alpaca and merino wools.
www.artesanoyarns.co.uk

Cascade Yarns
Manufacturers of a wide range of wools.
www.cascadeyarns.com

Coats and Crafts
Suppliers of Patons yarns.
www.coatscrafts.co.uk/Products/Knitting

Cygnet Yarns Ltd
UK-based manufacturer of yarn.
www.cygnetyarns.com

Designer Yarns
Providers of Debbie Bliss wools.
www.designeryarns.uk.com

Hooplayarn
Supplier of recycled cotton jersey yarn.
www.hooplayarn.co.uk

Jamieson's
Suppliers of Shetland wool.
www.jamiesonsofshetland.co.uk

Malabrigo Yarn
Providers of a range of wool in beautiful hand-dyed colors.
www.malabrigoyarn.com

Milla Mia
Manufacturers of DK-weight superwash merino wool.
www.millamia.com

Quince and Co.
Gorgeous yarns in a range of subtle colors and variety of weights.
quinceandco.com

Rico Design
A range of beautiful and affordable cotton and wool yarns.
www.rico-design.de

Rowan Yarns
Providers of a huge range of yarns in most weights and fibers.
www.knitrowan.com

Sublime Yarns/Sirdar Spinning Ltd
Manufacturers of both Sublime and Sirdar yarns.
www.sirdar.co.uk

Thomas B. Ramsden (Bradford) Limited
Suppliers of Wendy yarns.
www.tbramsden.co.uk

Yarn Love
Hand-dyed yarns in a huge array of colors and bases.
www.shopyarnlove.com

Zitron
Manufacturers of Trekking Tweed.
www.atelierzitron.de

OTHER CRAFT SUPPLIES

Yarns, Hooks, and Other Notions

UK
Loop Knitting
www.loopknittingshop.com

McA Direct
www.mcadirect.com

Australia
Morris and Sons
www.morrisandsons.com.au

The Wool Shack
www.thewoolshack.com

New Zealand
Knit World
www.knitting.co.nz

The Yarn Studio
www.theyarnstudio.co.nz

Wooden and Branch Buttons
Little Woodlanders
http://www.etsy.com/shop/
LittleWoodlanders

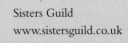

Children's clothing for photoshoots

Juicy Tots
www.juicytots.co.uk

Livie & Luca
www.livieandluca.co.uk

Love It Love It Love It
www.loveitloveitloveit.co.uk

Sisters Guild
www.sistersguild.co.uk

Tootsa MacGinty
www.tootsamacginty.com

Wild Things Funky Little Dresses
www.etsy.com/shop/wildthingsdresses

ACKNOWLEDGMENTS

Every time I pick up a book, the first thing I do is read the acknowledgements. The list of people says so much about the author and the process of bringing a book to life. My list of people is long, with so many people having left their mark on these pages.

Thank you first to my agent, Clare Hulton, whose belief in my work and desire to help left me over the moon at actually landing a deal. In fact, I still can't believe it.

To the wonderful staff at Kyle Books. Having long been a fan of their beautiful books, I am thrilled a work of mine is in the catalogue. Thank you Vicky, Nadine, Louise and all the others who made my book so beautiful.

Thank you to the models and their parents for allowing us to photograph their adorable children in my designs and to the yarn companies who generously gave yarn for use in the book: Artesano, Cascade Yarns, Cygnet, Designer Yarns, Malabrigo Yarns, Milla Mia, and Sublime/Sirdar.

My business partner, Kat Molesworth, for her unending wit and encouragement and for taking over much of the burden of the business while I wrote. She gave me the idea for the book in the first place: thank you!!

My technical editor, Joanne Scrace, deserves the highest praise for taking my patterns and turning them into something that makes sense. Many email and text messages, hundreds of tweets, a lot of brainstorming (the Sleepy Octopus and the Star Rug were her ideas), Joanne's patience and knowledge was a rock that gave me the confidence to design, knowing that she would be there to fix my mistakes.

To my friends, real and 'imaginary', who generously gave ideas, cake and unending support and patience as I dove head first into this huge task. So many people in real life and online pushed me not only to write the best book possible, but to believe that what I have to offer is worth reading, and I can never thank them enough.

My sister-in-law, Jessica Harrison, deserves a huge thank you for her help with sample making, as I would never have finished things in time! The brown Silver Birch Tunic and the Bunting Baby Blanket are her hard work.

To our parents, whose help and guidance supported us through a hectic summer of writing.

My three children, Ellis, Georgia, and Theo, who were (mostly) patient while Momma worked. Thank you, Ellis, for your tolerance as I promised yet again that I would play with you in five minutes/after this row/once the book is done. Georgia, thank you for staying relatively still as I measured and fitted and refitted so many different items. And Theo, thank you for only pouring coffee over my computer twice.

Last, and certainly most, Kevin. It is a gift to be with someone who believes in your work so thoroughly that they will make huge sacrifices to make it happen. Thank you doesn't even cover it. I love you, always.